MASON or ME

MASON or ME

How a Nice Guy Like Me Came to Loathe My Dog

Richard Mouw

TATE PUBLISHING & *Enterprises*

Mason or Me
Copyright © 2008 by Richard Mouw. All rights reserved.

This title is also available as a Tate Out Loud product. Visit www.tatepublishing.com for more information.

No part of this publication may be reproduced, stored in a retrieval system or transmitted in any way by any means, electronic, mechanical, photocopy, recording or otherwise without the prior permission of the author except as provided by USA copyright law.

Published by Tate Publishing & Enterprises, LLC
127 E. Trade Center Terrace | Mustang, Oklahoma 73064 USA
1.888.361.9273 | www.tatepublishing.com

Tate Publishing is committed to excellence in the publishing industry. The company reflects the philosophy established by the founders, based on Psalm 68:11,
"The Lord gave the word and great was the company of those who published it."

Book design copyright © 2008 by Tate Publishing, LLC. All rights reserved.
Cover design by Stefanie Rooney
Interior design by Joey Garrett

Published in the United States of America

ISBN: 978-1-60604-503-9
1. Biography & Autobiography: Personal
2. Pets: Dogs: General
08.06.23

DEDICATION

To Mason. Reluctantly.

TABLE OF CONTENTS

Introduction
9

First, the Facts
11

First Pets
15

The Perfect Dog
21

The Not-So-Perfect Dog
25

The Dog from Hell
31

The Interview
39

Buyer's Remorse
45

Quality of Life Adjustment
51

Odd Traits
55

Orifice Overload
59

Going Nautical
65

On a Walk
71

The Mason Calendar
75

Vacations
85

How Much Can a Man Take?
89

The Tummy Rub
93

More Lives than a Cat
97

Near Death Experience
103

Reconciliation
111

Afterword
115

INTRODUCTION

I have had dogs all my life, both by default and by choice. I have never loved and only once liked my dogs; for the most part, I simply tolerated their presence. I don't begrudge those who love their pets. To the contrary, I appreciate the bond between pet owners and their pets.

I do find it amusing, however, when dog owners vilify those who don't love dogs the way they do. There is great intolerance in the dog-owning community for those who do not share their love for their canine brethren, and many are seriously offended by cynical remarks about pets in general and dogs in particular. The thought of PETA people stalking me has crossed my mind, but I'm hoping that they have a sense of humor. Dogs appear to be happy, since tail wagging, licking, and barking all seem to me cheerful traits. Cats, on the other hand, strike me as crabby and somewhat snooty. Dogs beg you to pay attention to them, delighted by your mere presence, while cats allow you to approach only on their terms. That said, if I had to choose, I would take a cat over a dog any day of the week.

Aside from their fundamental happiness, however, everything else about dogs is offensive to me. If I needed some company or extra loving, I can think of any number of alternatives to getting a licking, drooling, barking, butt-dragging, digging, scratching, whining, vomit-eating dog. Having the love of a dog may be worth all this to some people, but count me out.

My opinion, of course, won't change anyone's mind about dogs, but that is not the point of this book. I have discovered over the years that a silent but large group of people share my opinion, while a vocal and even larger group of people despise my feelings about dogs. It is for both groups that I wrote this book, but it is the latter that made writing it so much fun.

FIRST, THE FACTS

When I thought about writing this little book, I knew that I would be treading on a sensitive subject. While I neither love nor hate dogs, I am probably in the minority simply by being neutral. No doubt some will construe my stories, comments, and recollections as those of a dog hater. I know this because even within my own relatively fair and balanced family I am accused of hating dogs.

You will see that in my journey through life, most of my encounters with dogs have been unpleasant. Frankly, it is quite remarkable that a man exposed to what I have experienced has retained his sanity. Despite these negative experiences, I put the needs and desires of my family ahead of my own and purchased a dog—not just once, but twice—in both cases to substantial self-detriment. I say this not to blow my own horn or to gain your sympathy but to show that I am not as bad as you might think upon first glance.

Let me go on record as saying I do not hate dogs. In fact, I really like some dogs. Just the other day I passed a man walking his St. Bernard puppy. I stopped the man, commented on how cute his puppy was, and proceeded to pet it. While I did not talk "puppy talk" (Oh-watta-a-coot-puppy or Gimme-kissy), I did genuinely enjoy petting the puppy and will even acknowledge that it was in fact quite adorable. Another time some friends purchased a golden retriever. Their young kids were eager to have us come over and see their new puppy, and I was happy to oblige. The dog was cute and soft, and I readily admit that I enjoyed holding it. My own kids still talk about the time when our dog (the one I'm about to tell you about) was a puppy and slept next to me while I napped. I don't recall the incident, but they have photo proof, so why deny it? Real men can like puppies, and I admittedly have a soft spot for babies, even baby dogs.

I realize that these positive experiences were with puppies and not dogs, but I'm sure there are some dogs I like as well. While none come to mind at the moment, I can confidently say that I would like them if they meet the following criteria:

1. They belong to someone else.
2. They are out of earshot.
3. They never come to my house.

But even if I did hate all dogs, so what? When did that become a crime? Animal abuse is a crime, but not liking them should not relegate one to the bottom rung of humanity. People hate other people all the time, are sometimes even applauded for it, so why does it irk so many people to hear that a person doesn't like dogs?

The truth is I only hate my own dog. You will see that I direct my anger and frustration to just that one creature—in my opinion, rightly so. This single dog has nearly put me over the edge on many occasions, and you will conclude, as

I have, that the dog has serious mental issues that are detrimental to those around him.

As I recall, a dog is supposed to be man's best friend. Best friends are kind, considerate, accommodating, and understanding. Friends who demonstrate these traits receive friendship in return, and together they form a lifelong bond. My own dog has demonstrated none of these traits toward me despite the fact that I reached out to him from the very start. Instead of a lifelong bond of friendship, I have only lifelong bondage.

Friendship must be a two-way street. When it is not, either indifference or animosity will develop. I have tried indifference and have been quite literally dumped on, so I have developed a deep-seated animosity toward the dog that I so graciously brought into my home. Over the years, I have threatened to walk out if we didn't deal with the dog issue. At times, life was becoming unbearable, and it seemed quite pointless to even have a dog. Every time I laid it on the line and gave the family the choice between Mason or me, however, they would either ignore me or tell me to enjoy my new life. So much for the dad being the *head of the household*.

It became clear that allowing the family to choose between the dog and the dad would not result in a favorable outcome for me, so I had to resort to clandestine schemes to achieve my goal. The following is an account of how it came down to Mason or me and how I had to take matters into my own hands to rid myself of the menace.

FIRST PETS

I think it is safe to say that very few of us didn't have pets at some point in our lives, and I suspect that most people can remember what that first pet was. It may have been a cat, hamster, dog, or goldfish, but most people will remember at least the pet's name. My son's first pets were four goldfish, and he affectionately named them One, Two, Orange, and White. It was easy to figure out which one was White, but only my son knew how to sort out the other three.

My daughter had hamsters named Gizmo and Sherman. The most memorable thing about Sherman was that he bit. In fact, as the family gathered around the burial hole at the backyard memorial service after Sherman died, my three-year-old son offered the only worthwhile eulogy: "At least he had good teeth." Hamsters are among the most pointless pets. They smell, are dirty, have to be caged, and rarely let you hold them. In addition to those outstanding qualities, you get to listen to that squeaky wheel that they seem to use only when you're trying to sleep. Advice to new parents: never get your kids a hamster or guinea pig. You will regret it.

My wife grew up with Chester the sheepdog and later a large poodle named Cocoa. She also had a small pony, complete with a miniature barn in the backyard next to the swimming pool. Even though they lived in a subdivision, my father-in-law, who grew up in Chicago, wanted to create the appearance of life on the farm on his half-acre lot. As I understand it, when he saw his kids riding sawhorses, he decided it would be nice to have a real horse. One day he pulled up in the station wagon, dragged a live pony out of the backseat, and presto! Instant farm.

The names of our pets come complete with stories, each remembered through the experiences of a child enthralled with that first pet. The stories are usually quite similar, but rarely did we actually spend much time with our pets or make much effort to care for them. We remember wonderful times with them, but in reality, we pretty much ignored them after those first few days. Care for the pet nearly always falls on Mom; if it weren't for her, most pets wouldn't last a week. Case in point: one of our kids had a pet bunny, appropriately named Mr. Bunny. One day my wife was on the phone and glanced toward the window to see Mr. Bunny being dragged at the end of a leash by our four-year-old, who skipped merrily along, "taking it for a walk."

My own experience with pets dates back to when I was about eight. We named our first dog Snoopy. Since the cartoon strip *Peanuts* was popular back then, I assume we named him after the infamous Red Baron though he was a black poodle. The only thing I remember was seeing him sleeping on top of Dad while he took a nap. It always reminded me of *Hop on Pop*. Something traumatic must have happened to Snoopy because all of a sudden he was gone.

He may have died or been evicted from the family for some reason the parents wanted to keep from us, but that is all I remember about Snoopy. He was black, he slept, and he was gone, which is another common pet phenomenon. We tend to remember getting them, maybe the memory of an event or two, but generally we're a bit foggy when it comes to the exit strategy.

The childhood pet I remember best and that was with us the longest was named Iky (i-kee). An odd name, to be sure, but he was named after President Eisenhower, who my mom felt was deserving of a namesake. I remember getting the dog. He was a white poodle—poodles were the "in" dog back then, long before Shih Tzus were invented and certainly before it was acceptable to say Shih Tzu—and my sister and I were responsible for picking the name.

I vividly remember sitting down with my sister and listing the names we felt were suitable for the new puppy. Her first choice was Whitey, which I felt was a bit bland but not a bad attempt for a four-year-old trying to name a white dog. (Ironically, she grew up to be the creative one.) Being the elder sibling and recipient of the coveted birthright, I nixed the name. Anything was better than Whitey, and my list included manly dog names—Lassie, Bo, and Ranger, all quite suitable for a miniature toy poodle in our family home. These were not good enough for my mom, however, and she pulled rank. Her affections for Eisenhower won the day. Iky it was.

Iky must have been a reasonably good dog because I have no particularly negative memories of him. I remember that Dad would come home, walk through the door, and start clapping his hands, getting the dog revved up to the point where he would bark uncontrollably. This was the signal for Iky to begin running frantic figure eights around the island

and kitchen table, doing that excited growling dog thing while going Mach 4. I never liked the barking, and to this day I think all dogs should have corrective vocal cord surgery. There is absolutely no reason for a dog to bark, unless of course he is a watchdog, but even a barkless watchdog would have what really matters: his teeth.

I don't recall ever really wanting the dog, but I am sure I must have, just like most kids. Besides, in the 1970s it seemed to be expected that families had pets. Nearly everyone had a dog or cat back then, and it really did not matter if there was love for the pet. As far as I was concerned, Iky could just as well have been a chair: convenient if needed, but otherwise forgettable sitting there in the corner.

In exchange for a curly-haired pet that barked and smelled, we were required to feed, pet, coddle, let out, pick up poop from, and otherwise take care of the pet. Even then I didn't think it sounded like a fair trade, but that was the tradeoff for having a dog. Of course, rarely did any kids live up to the agreement, and by default Mom most often performed the obligatory chores.

Iky was your typical family pet. You let him out and then had to coax him to come back in. I can remember trying to call him back in during the middle of winter and getting quite upset when he would not come back. On numerous occasions I would slip on my winter boots, walk outside at 7 o'clock in the morning shouting, "Iky, Come!" "Iky, Come!" That's when I was eight. When I was fourteen it became "Iky, Come, you stupid dog!" For the life of me, I can't understand why a skinny short-haired dog takes twenty minutes sniffing for the right place to pee when it's ten degrees out—especially when they eventually use the same spot anyway. They go through the motions as if it was a really big deal, but in the end it is just a show designed to make you think there is some sort of plan or instinct involved. I get the part about instinct, but sheesh... just get on with it. To me it indicates how dumb dogs really are. How hard is it to find the same yellow spot day after day, *especially* when there is snow on the ground?

My dad was always proud of his lawn. He really enjoyed keeping it nice, especially since he had me around to run the mower and do the dirty work. I had to cut the lawn twice a week, with the bag, and be sure I cut tight to the edging. (Had I not been there to cut the lawn, I suspect his standards would have relaxed.) Nevertheless, I was the "lawn guy," responsible for the aesthetics of the yard. As the lawn guy, my job description also included disposing of the dog poop. While Iky was not big, he was frequent, and there was always poop to deal with.

We obtained a pooper-scooper to assist with the task. You remember the pooper-scooper, don't you? It was an ingenious device having two wooden handles with a metal scoop at the end of each handle. Nowadays people use the more advanced disposable plastic gloves, but in the 70s, you needed the pooper-scooper, which allowed you to deal with the matter from three feet away. Thankfully, we never walked the dog, because it would have been quite inconvenient to haul the pooper-scooper on every excursion. No, Iky stayed close to home and pooped only in the yard. The poop did need to be picked up regularly, however, for the integrity of the lawn. I didn't really care about the lawn, but I did care about the consequences of doing a poor job, and so I picked up the poop. Hence the pooper-scooper. If I hadn't been there to tend to things, I suspect there would have been no pooper-scooper and, by extension, no manicured lawn. In retrospect, I think it is a very real possibility that if Dad had

had to deal with the poop, Iky would have had a shorter stay at our home.

Eventually all good things must come to an end, and life with Iky was about to change. One morning during my junior year in high school, Iky had an untimely run-in with a car in front of our house. Since my dad was at work, I was the next male in line, so Mom called on me to deal with the situation. With blanket in hand and Mom and the siblings watching anxiously from the living room window, I scooped Iky up from the street and took him to the vet on my way to school. The vet said that he could sew him up, but the dog would likely never be the same. He advised putting him down, and that's all I needed to hear; besides, I was late for school. We never got another dog while I was at home, and I never missed having one.

THE PERFECT DOG

The first home my wife and I owned was a small house on several acres tucked into the woods. It was a great setting: woods, pond, and seclusion—the perfect *Little House on the Prairie* homestead. It was also the perfect property for a dog, and the intoxication of land ownership made all my negative childhood memories of dog ownership disappear. I was suddenly a dog lover. It was only natural for a Grizzly Adams type of man who lived in the woods and worked the land to own a big outdoor dog. I grew up with the poodle Iky, and my wife grew up with one of those large mutant-looking poodles with the contoured haircuts, so it was maybe a bit unusual for both of us to want a tough outdoor dog. However, for whatever reason, we both agreed that a collie was the dog for us.

We found a place south of town that raised collies; it was literally a collie farm. There were dozens of full-grown collies of all types running around. It was quite intimidating, and I feared being attacked if I got out of the car, so I asked my wife to go to the door first. Dogs of all sorts love her, and since they usually don't like me, I felt there was no reason to risk being attacked when she could safely make the introductions. Once the owner cleared the bodyguard of dogs out of the way, we were ushered into the puppy barn. Even I have to admit that puppies are cute, and like my wife, I instantly fell in love with dozens of tail-wagging collie puppies.

There were pups of all types and sizes; sable and white, black and white, and blue merles are the only types of collies I am aware of, and all were available. Aside from color they all looked pretty much the same and we selected our particular puppy, a sable-and-white model that was a few weeks from being weaned.

We headed home, proud of our purchase and feeling as if we were about to have a baby. We readied the home for our new puppy: doghouse, dog dishes, blankets, food, and enough chew toys to last a doggie lifetime. After the puppy was weaned, we took him home and showered him with round-the-clock attention, not necessarily because we wanted to but because he required it. Like babies, puppies are up during the night crying and need to be held, cleaned, or fed for those first few weeks.

Callie, as we named him, was home for only a short time when he suddenly became very ill. He was lethargic and uninterested in food, and he grew very weak. I am quite sure it wasn't for lack of proper care, since we absolutely spoiled that dog.

We took him to the vet, and he ended up spending a week in the vet hospital being nursed back to health. It was an intestinal affliction that nearly took him out. I liked to think he came with the ailment as opposed to picking it up while in our care. We still remember Dr. Munroe; if it were not for him, Callie would have been only a brief memory.

But thanks to Dr. Munroe, Callie was soon back home getting the lay of the land at our little home in the woods.

From the start, we kept Callie the Collie, as we soon began calling him, outside. We had a large insulated doghouse, the mother of all doghouses in size, construction, and amenities. This house had a chalet roof and fully insulated walls and floor. It was doghouse overkill.

The sump pump in the basement of our the home ran every ten minutes, constantly delivering fresh water to the pond, located only a few yards from the doghouse. Even in winter, the pond never completely froze due to the continuous flow of fresh water, making it an ever-ready source of drinking water for the dog. The only required dog maintenance was putting food in the dog dish on the deck each morning, and even the need for that was probably in question, since the dog was quite adept at killing wild animals.

So, Callie was practically self-sufficient and virtually maintenance-free, save for the periodic trip to the vet for shots. Even that would not have happened were it not for my wife. Let's face it, dogs have roamed the earth for millennia without the need for shots, and they seem to have done just fine.

What made Callie even more special was that we never had to tie him up. He was a homebody, to the point where we couldn't even take him for a walk. He simply would not leave the woods. He also rarely barked and then only when treeing a raccoon or catching a possum. Callie was a dog's dog and barked only in life-threatening situations, not at squirrels, mailmen, and walkers. He would often catch his prey, and while he wouldn't hurt a person, the fact that he could rip a possum to shreds implied at least a certain amount of protection for us living in the woods.

We owned a dog that would not run away, would not

chase cars, didn't bark unnecessarily, stayed outdoors, and needed food only periodically. Callie was without question the perfect dog. When I worked outside, he would be nearby, giving me the companionship of man's best friend but never requiring me to acknowledge him. Callie clearly loved his independent life, so it was only appropriate that when we moved, we sold him with the house. We told the buyers that Callie was part of the deal. The new owners picked up where we left off, and I suspect Callie the Collie never even noticed the change. Letting a pet remain at the place he loves while you move away takes true love, I believe, and I was honored to give that sort of love. The new owners sent us a card some years later telling us that Callie had died at a ripe old dog age on the land he loved.

THE NOT-SO-PERFECT DOG

A couple of years after we adopted Callie, my wife decided that he needed a friend. She claimed he was lonely all by himself out there in the woods and needed a dog companion to keep him company. I suspect this was a misdirected maternal instinct since we didn't yet have children. I can understand wanting a playmate for an only child, but I don't know that a dog would really care, especially in Callie's case. I suspect no dog in the history of dog-kind had it as nice as he did, and I can't imagine Callie wanting to share his little slice of heaven with another dog. I know that I wouldn't want to share all those perks if I were a dog. Nevertheless, my wife was convinced this was necessary, and so we embarked on a dog search.

We determined right away that we wanted a little variety, so we would go for something other than a collie. We wanted another large dog, and we landed on a yellow lab as the dog of choice. We were given the name of a reputable dog breeder whose own yellow lab was about to have puppies. When the puppies were born, we picked the one we wanted, which essentially amounted to reaching in and grabbing one. As I recall, every one of the puppies looked identical and you couldn't go wrong regardless of the selection.

We named our new puppy Cruger, which had no special meaning. Actually, it had no meaning at all. We just liked the name and the phrase "Callie and Cruger," which had a kind of sitcom ring to it. Cruger came home and stayed in the house until he was old enough to move into the great outdoors with Callie. The adjustment was really quite easy for the two dogs, primarily because of the easygoing nature of Callie.

Cruger was a wild thing. Like all puppies, he had to chew and jump on everything, and when he took up permanent residence outside with Callie, he learned quickly who was in charge. Callie did have his limits and occasionally had to put Cruger in his place when he went too far, which in the beginning was quite often. We set up a second doghouse next to Callie's, and there was no misunderstanding as to who was the new kid on the block. Cruger settled in nicely and began learning the ropes from Callie.

Unfortunately, Cruger did not have the homebody instinct of Callie and soon was wandering outside the property limits at will. What made things worse is that the dog was getting quite large and therefore intimidating. This dog had shoulders as broad as my own, and while I'm admittedly not the Hulk, even my shoulders are big by dog standards. Cruger was incredibly friendly, but anyone who has ninety pounds of dog bounding from the woods toward them is naturally going to be scared. The dog really didn't have any faults except for his wandering habits, but we were getting complaints and had to deal with him.

Cindy with Cruger and Callie

Tying the dog up did not sit well, especially since we were so spoiled with Callie's behavior. But it seemed the only way to deal with the wandering menace, and so we proceeded to build a dog run. Since we had the space, I stretched a thirty-foot-long cable between two trees and then gave Cruger another fifteen feet of lead attached to a pulley that rolled along the main cable. As a further precaution against injuring the dog I attached massive springs on all ends of the cables in order to cushion the effect any time he ran to the end of the line. The dog run was finished and impressive.

Cruger spent his days and nights attached to the lead and didn't seem to mind at all. But we weren't having any fun.

We really couldn't enjoy him because every time we untied him he flew off into the woods, never to return if it were up to him. In addition, he was a barker and spent his days barking at anything that moved in the woods. I suspect a lot of this had to do with him still being a puppy, although we might have to take some blame for not knowing how to train him. *Our bad*. But the goal of providing a buddy for Callie was not accomplished since Cruger annoyed Callie as much as he annoyed us. We agreed that the Cruger acquisition was a mistake, but now what?

As luck would have it, my wife saw an article on leader dogs and found that yellow labs were high on the list of desirable dogs for this program. We debated on whether this was even worth a shot, since we couldn't imagine how anyone would be able to tame this savage beast. Yet it seemed worth a try, since acceptance into the program would be beneficial for us, for Cruger, and for his prospective new owner.

We contacted Leader Dogs for the Blind and received the necessary paperwork. Based on Cruger's age, size, pedigree, etc., they were willing to take a look at him. We had to take him to the other side of the state for enrollment, which was quite an inconvenience with my work schedule. Rather than taking him myself, I had one of our drivers at work drop him off on the way to making a delivery in the area. Imagine Cruger cooped up in the cab of a truck for four hours with a complete stranger. To this day I can't believe how bold I was in making such a request.

The truck driver was willing and left early one morning on his run, Cruger riding shotgun. Later that day I received a call from my driver: Cruger had been rejected due to a sore on his ear. Until that healed he could not be considered. These people were fussy. So, back home came Cruger, having spent a long day driving around Michigan in the cab of a truck. While the driver was not happy, we were thrilled that they were considering the dog at all. Some weeks later, after the sore healed, we tried again, and this time he was accepted into the program.

I don't remember what our backup plan was if Cruger failed the program and had to be returned, but he didn't return, and we didn't hear from Leader Dogs for the Blind for nearly a year. Then one day we received a picture of Cruger standing erect and quite dignified next to a man in a suit. The man was a judge, and Cruger was now spending his days in a courtroom using his new skills as a leader dog. Of all the dog experiences I have had in my life, this is the story with the happiest ending.

THE DOG FROM HELL

Some people think that all dogs are sweet, but that has not been my experience. In my opinion, there are tolerable dogs, and then there are those that could be compared to the devil himself. Maybe my experience with Callie set a benchmark that no other dog could possibly attain. After all, when you've had the perfect dog, nothing else really has a fair chance. If Callie was the perfect dog, and Cruger was the less-than-perfect dog, then our next dog was about eight notches further down the scale. In the brief time we had this dog, the groundwork was laid for years of bad dog experiences that helped shape my negative opinion of dogs.

After we moved, we went several years without getting another dog. It was an easy adjustment, and the couple of times we needed a dog fix, all we had to do was walk a quarter mile through the woods to the old homestead and visit Callie. Then we had kids, and events came full circle. When the kids started getting a bit older, they began lobbying for a dog. We delayed as long as we could, with substitutions of fish, bunnies, hamsters, and even reptiles, but it was a dog that they truly wanted. Only a cute puppy would satisfy them.

Had it not been for our daughter, we probably would never have gotten a dog. She was the persistent one, and when she wants something, she doesn't give up. She brought it up at dinner, slipped notes under our pillows, and got weepy when talking about the joys that a puppy would bring. You would think that a couple of adults with the experiences we had would know what we were getting into and would have held fast. In retrospect, it would have been so easy to say no, live with a few tears, and move on to years of greater happiness. But like most parents we caved, and in the end we gave in out of exhaustion.

Based on our experience with the lesser mammals, I knew where the whole dog thing would end up. The kids would promise to do their part to care for it, they would shower it with attention for the first three days, and then they would promptly forget about it and move on to the next thing. Anticipating what proved to be correct, I determined that there was no need for us to spend a cent on a dog when we could get all kinds of them free at the local dog shelter. A dog is a dog, and the kids would think any puppy was cute, so why not go on the cheap?

Our criteria were minimal. We wanted a small to medium-size dog that didn't shed and wouldn't be wild. We went to the shelter and, as expected, found a cute puppy, black with white patches and a white circle around one eye. The resident dog expert assured us that the puppy we selected would get no bigger than knee high, would have short hair, and would not be high-strung. I wrongly assumed that the people at the dog shelter knew their dogs; certainly there had to be training in the sciences of animals and genetics required to become a dog shelter worker. I should have looked for the diploma because she was either misinformed or lying or God was having fun with us, since within six months Chipper, as we named him, weighed ninety pounds, had long hair that fell out in clumps, and knocked the kids to the floor every time he greeted them.

Pardon my French, but to say that Chipper seemed like the dog from hell would not be an overstatement. I know it is unkind to refer to any of God's creatures that way, but in this case it was true. To start with, it is not possible for a dog to shed any more than Chipper did. The hair was long, course, and abundant—and ended up everywhere, even though the dog was restricted to the tile-floored kitchen. The dog could not stay outdoors or in the garage because he would bark uncontrollably, and no amount of discipline would change that behavior. Even the Dog Whisperer would be baffled with this one and would likely have given up.

Then there was the matter of the kids. Letting the kids play with Chipper was as good as handing them a death sentence, since every time he got near them he bowled them over, thinking it was fun. He was just a stupid dog who did not understand that he was six times bigger than the children. He would launch ninety pounds of friendly fire at anyone under ten. While outdoors in the winter, he would body slam the nearest kid, grab his hat, and run pell-mell with it until I tackled him to retrieve it. This dog was so big he once stopped briefly mid-stride to throw up a gym sock he had eaten and then continued his activities, smiling all the while. Yes, this dog smiled.

We installed an electric dog fence to keep him at bay, and while I initially enjoyed coaxing him over it just to see his reaction, he seemed to enjoy the jolt he got when he crossed the wire and began crossing it of his own free will. Every time he escaped, we faced a moral dilemma. While the thought of him running away for good was enjoyable, we feared for the lives of the neighborhood kids, who would likely get bowled over in the process. By encouraging him to cross the electric fence, I had created a dog monster.

Then there was the lawn. Chipper absolutely loved digging large holes in the yard, and he could have dug circles around the Digging-est Dog of children's book fame. While we had acres of woods around the house, he of course would dig only in the yard. This naturally didn't sit well with me because of the pride I took in the lawn, a trait I honed in my younger years. It took some time, but eventually I did succumb to the allure of a manicured lawn. I think that dads who have fine lawns beget boys that like fine lawns, although I'm not sure if it's a genetic trait or a desire that stems from years of forced mowing.

Chipper in a rare subdued moment

Whatever the cause, I liked my nice lawn and worked hard to keep it that way. Whether it was weeds, moles, tire tracks, or digging dogs, all assailants of my lawn were sworn enemies. Every time I'd find Chipper digging, I'd catch him—which in itself was an ordeal—and yell myself hoarse trying to get through to his little brain that digging was against the rules. He would just sit there, wagging his tail, with drool dribbling out of his smiling mouth.

There were times when my treatment of Chipper might have looked questionable. For example, when I kicked the dog, I was in fact just trying to get his attention. A kick to Chipper was like a back rub; he actually seemed to enjoy it. Frankly, I think we both benefited from these episodes, since I was able to act out my anger at Chipper, and he got what he considered to be a massage. In all honesty, this dog could not be hurt or trained, and was for all practical purposes worthless. My wife claims that I will answer to God one day for the way I treated Chipper, and I'm sure she's right, but doggone it, that dog was evil.

What was nearly as bad as the holes in the lawn were the circles of dead grass that were the result of his pee. Up until Chipper, I wasn't sure whether it was male or female dogs whose urine killed grass. Let there be no question that it is the male. Chipper's pee was nuclear, and the circles of dead grass combined with the holes he dug made my once-manicured lawn look like the surface of the moon. It was both dreadful and an embarrassment.

In the time we had him, there was really only one sweet Chipper story worth repeating, and it didn't even really involve Chipper. It was my daughter's concern over the neutering process, which in her mind was like a mutilation (which was probably accurate in Chipper's case, given how big he was). She referred to it as "noodling," which tells you how much a five-year-old really understands about the process. We dragged out the "noodling" story as long as we could, as it was one of those ongoing fountains of entertainment every time she said it. I recall hearing somewhere along the way that neutering a dog tends to calm him down. "Noodling" Chipper didn't calm him down or slow him down. It was like a non-event to him, and he bounded out of the car after the procedure as if nothing had happened.

We didn't keep Chipper for even a year, since it wouldn't have been long before he would have destroyed our home, our kids, our marriage, and our sanity. Even my wife was on board to get rid of him, but we faced the kid dilemma. Despite his shortcomings—which were all he had—the kids still loved Chipper, or more likely they loved the concept of having him, since they really didn't pay any attention to him for fear of being maimed. Again, looking back I wonder why we didn't just get rid of him, listen to a day or two of crying, and move on. Nobody would have suffered any permanent emotional trauma as a result.

But we spent agonizing days trying to think of a way to get rid of the dog and pacify the kids. I would have shot the dog or taken him for the clichéd ride in the country, but burying him would have required a lot of work and stealth, not to mention the size hole that would have been required. I would have spent more time digging the hole than I had ever spent actually paying attention to the dog. Plus, putting him in my car would have jeopardized the upholstery. Chipper in the car was the same as Chipper on the lawn, only on steroids, and no seat cover was safe. Thankfully, my wife came up with the solution that finally rid us of Chipper, but even that didn't go smoothly.

The easy solution would have been simply to return him to the dog shelter, which is what I would have done as my second choice. But my wife thought that the least we could do was find a home where the poor dog would be loved, as impossible as that seemed to be. The last thing she was going to do was take Chipper back to the shelter, where he very likely would be put down. She is a sucker for guilt and has a soft spot in her heart as big as, well, as big as Chipper.

Creatively telling the kids that we were going to "trade Chipper in" on a smaller dog, she placed a classified ad. The well-worded ad in the paper prompted a call from an interested family. The ad read something like "Large indoor dog that is exceptionally friendly and loves kids. *Free* to a good home." In a general sense, the ad was true, even though she was technically lying through her teeth. Her sins found her out, however, since the family that excitedly took Chipper off our hands called the next day and wanted to return him. Apparently, in that one night Chipper destroyed their house, made their kids cry, and generally disrupted family life, conclusive proof that the problem was the dog, not the dog's owners.

Chipper was coming back, but for the sake of our credibility and sanity, it was imperative that the kids didn't find out. They had accepted the reality of Chipper being gone and were anticipating a new puppy. Therefore, my wife picked up Chipper and apologized to the people for the damage he had caused to house and home, suggesting that they call their insurance agent. Wanting to be done with the completely depressing episode, she promptly drove him to the dog shelter whence he came. Dead dog or not, the matter had to end.

Months later we continued to tell the kids that Chipper was happy at his new home on the other side of town, knowing full well that he was likely digging holes in that big yard in the sky. Imagine our surprise when, nearly a year later, the kids spotted Chipper, now named Joshua, with his new owner in the dog shelter newsletter. The new owner described "Joshua" as a super dog, great with kids and a joy to have around, which could only have meant the guy was lying through his teeth. Thankfully, kids' memories are short, so we didn't have to explain how Chipper ended up at the dog shelter and then with his new owner rather than with that nice family on the other side of town. All that mattered to them was that he was alive and well.

THE INTERVIEW

After Chipper's reassignment, it was time to live up to our agreement to get another dog. Given our experience, anything would be better than Chipper, and I was open to whatever the family wanted. Shucks, at this point I would happily have taken a pit bull over a dog like Chipper. I'd much rather live with the danger of pit bull teeth than the aggravation and annoyance of Chipper.

My wife had been doing some research on the ideal dog. Her research was very thorough, based both on interviews she conducted with neighboring pet owners and on hearsay from people who didn't have a clue what they were talking about. This group included former dog owners who regretted ever having owned one and wanted others to share their pain, and those who had never owned a dog but knew of someone who had. It's like with all things: just because someone has something, we think they're an authority on the subject. Every seasoned salesperson will tell you that this is simply a defense mechanism. The owner of the lemon car would never admit that the car was a piece of junk because by doing so they are admitting that they were suckered into buying it. Don't kid yourself. People who say they love their dogs are likely just as miserable as I was with Chipper... they just don't have the guts to admit it. At least I'm honest. Unfortunately, happy or not, we went to current dog owners for advice.

If someone had what she thought was a cute dog, my wife needed to know everything about it and find out where it came from. Many of these "cute" breeds come from dog farms, as I like to call them, and while they produce different types of dogs, the farms themselves seem to be essentially the same; lots of dogs, and lots of noise. We looked at several types of dogs, and one breed—or "brand," as I prefer to call it—in particular caught her eye. I'll call this particular brand the "Sham" dog. As I understand it, the Sham dog is part something, combined with another part something, with a dash of something else thrown in a generation or so back. In other words, it's a mutt with a pedigree. I've learned that cute dogs are in one category and ugly dogs in another. Both categories have loud, obnoxious, biting, and otherwise annoying dogs, but only the cute ones are worthy of being considered a "breed." As with people, the good-looking ones get more hall passes than the ugly ones. I don't need to be a dog expert to know that mixing breeds creates a mutt. You can call it any fancy name you want, but at the end of the day it is no less a mutt than the neighborhood stray that isn't quite as cute.

Upon further researching the Sham brand, my wife discovered that they breed the Shams to create the types of traits you want. No shedding? No problem. High-strung. Low-keyed. You decide and they will breed it. Essentially, you simply put in your order, and they select the parents, mating time, and, I assume, frequency, and a few months later out comes your specified dog, perfect in every way. It supposedly takes a specially trained expert with additional forecasting skills to predict the exact makeup of the dog. I'm not sure which college you go to for training in dog genetics, but they sure have this process down to a science. (It's probably the same college that the folks at the dog shelter attended.)

Our requirements amounted to everything that Chipper was not. We needed a non-barking, non-shedding, low-keyed, loveable, likeable, good-with-kids small dog that would double as a quasi watchdog that would provide some degree of safety for our family that lived in the woods. Imagine my surprise in learning that these particular traits were a specialty of Sham dogs. Maybe my luck with dogs was changing.

Normally you simply go to the dog store, pet shop, or pet owner wanting to get rid of puppies and make your purchase. Not so with Sham dogs. I discovered that we needed to be interviewed, much as you would be when adopting a child. Yes, an interview was required to determine if we were a suitable family for such a *tailored brand...* excuse me, breed of mutt as the Sham dog. Normally I would have thrown back my head and laughed, uttered an expletive or two, and then moved on to the next option. But I was committed to delivering what the family wanted as penance for what we now refer to as the Chipper Affair. Therefore, I agreed to the interview. (Note once again my selfless love of family.)

We made an appointment, and the Sham dog people made it very clear that the entire family was required to attend and, I presumed, pass the interview. My kids instructed me to lie through my teeth when asked to speak, but to remain quiet whenever possible.

"Dad, don't say a *thing* to mess this up!" said my son, who was twelve at the time. I clearly had the power to make or break the deal; in retrospect, I should have capitalized on this power and let it slip that I didn't want a dog. But I submitted to the family's demands and paid a price for my compliance.

We arrived at the dog farm—which is what these places are—and had a brief look at the puppies. These people are smart. They know that all puppies, like babies, are cute. (There are plenty of ugly dogs, but has anyone ever seen an ugly puppy? A lot like people, isn't it!?) They have learned that once you see the puppies you'll agree to anything in the interview, so it really isn't a fair setting.

We proceeded with the interview, but in all honesty, I remember very little of what was said. I do remember thinking I must be on *Candid Camera*. I couldn't believe that I was actually being interviewed to buy a dog. It felt a lot like having to buy a membership to *spend* money at Sam's Club. My cynicism must have gotten in the way of objectivity because all I could think about was how stupid the whole process was. I imagined being on the outside watching as the seller tried to determine if we had the dog-raising skills suitable for this exclusive brand of dog. This was all part of the marketing plan and justification for the obscene amount of money they wanted for something they had nothing to do with. Two dogs mate and twelve weeks later there are puppies. "Six hundred dollars, please."

Fortunately for the family, I somehow managed to evade the tough questions, and we did in fact pass the interview. Of course, who are they kidding? For that amount of money, I'll bet they let anybody have the dog. The interview and qualification process simply build the desirability of the brand in the dog community. It's all marketing. You would assume that when you took the Sham dog home and showed it to your friends and neighbors, they would say, "Wow, how did you even *qualify* for a Sham dog interview? You are so lucky! If only I could have a Sham dog." Of course, most of the friends and neighbors laughed their butts off when they heard I'd submitted to an interview and then forked over the money for any dog, let alone a Sham dog.

So far, we had reviewed the puppy pen, passed the interview, and were now going back to the pen to select our dog. We first had to review the criteria once again: a non-barking, non-shedding, low-keyed, loveable, likeable, good-with-kids small dog that would double as a quasi watchdog that would provide some degree of safety for our family that lived in the woods. I was pleased to hear that this would be an easy order to fill, but there were still a few features to determine. "How big would you like it and in what color?" were the next questions. It was like shopping for a pair of pants at Kohl's. As I've said, they apparently have the genetic code of Sham dogs mapped out further than we do with people. The Shammers, as I now call them, can literally design your dream dog to fill your specific needs and wants.

Imagine our surprise and good fortune when we learned that the exact dog we wanted was in stall number three, only weeks away from being weaned and ready to take home. What a stroke of good fortune. It could only be sheer providence that this particular puppy was going to be placed in our very home at this exact time. *Oh*, the wonder of it all. I pretended to be elated, until I saw the price tag: six hundred dollars for a dog, and a mutt at that?! What a scam... I mean Sham. However, after my post—Chipper Affair commitment to the family, the walk in the dog pen, the interview, and then the selection of our dream dog, there was no way I could nix this deal and remain in good standing with the family. Besides, given the alternative, I'd have given my retirement fund for anything but Chipper, even a Sham dog. I was committed.

The final requirement to purchase this dog was to sign the purchase agreement. Yes, a purchase agreement to buy a dog. Among other things, we had to agree to provide a good home for the dog, agree to never breed it, pay to have the dog fixed at the appropriate time, never sell it or give it away without permission, and report to the breeders when the dog died. This appeared more like a lease than a purchase, but I signed the agreement, wrote the check, and took the family home. I had spent more time shopping for a dog than I had for our house, and I had had enough. Besides, if they thought I was going to do any of those things I'd agreed to, they were crazy. What were they going to do, sue me to get the dog back? I'd kill to have a notice demanding that I give the dog back or else…

I left thinking that I had just been a victim of fraud. I could not believe I had paid six hundred dollars for a dog I didn't want, to give to kids who would never take care of it, in order to provide enjoyment that would never be realized. In the process, I had been interrogated, humiliated, and fleeced. Still, I had fulfilled my commitment and now had about three weeks to contemplate my actions before Sham dog moved into our home

BUYER'S REMORSE

In the weeks between selection and acquisition, we settled on the name Mason for our new dog. There was no real story behind the name, except that my wife liked it and the kids agreed. It was a collaborative process. My father-in-law wanted to name it "Milton," since his name was Hamilton. With lukewarm reception, he suggested "Hogan," only because he liked the sound of it and was always a *Hogan's Heroes* fan. One of the kids wanted to name it "Racin' Mason" since the dog looked as if he could run fast. I suggested "Mason Dixon," again trying to play off the dominant Mason theme and at the same time look as if I cared. In the end, the official name of our Sham dog was "Racin' Mason Dixon Milton Hogan Mouw"—Mason, for short.

While Mason looked the part of a cute, cuddly dog, he was anything but. During the interview, we never thought about ordering a dog that didn't nip or bite... it was kind of assumed that a custom-bred high-priced family dog wouldn't bite. Unfortunately, this was not the case with Mason, and from the very start this dog had a temper that continues to lash out to this day.

Bringing Mason home

We have no idea where all his pent-up anger came from. Given the intensity of the interview process and the price tag of the dog, one would assume that this wasn't a result of abuse at the dog farm. (Getting $600 a dog should be incentive enough for the owners to properly care for their investment.) From what we could see, his siblings didn't pick on him either. They all looked and acted the same, and none seemed to be lacking for anything. The only explanation for Mason's temper can be that it is in his genes, but clearly a gene that wasn't evident until he was weaned and in his new home; so much for the superior breeding process of Sham dogs. We soon learned that we had been sold a lemon, in more respects than one.

Mason adapted to our family quickly, and we never knew there was a problem until the first friends started to arrive to check out the new dog. The minute someone would reach out to pet Mason, he would step back, roll back his lower lip and let out a growl that said, "Touch me and I'll bite your hand off!" This became the rule and not the exception, and while he warmed up to an occasional stranger, it was rare. Were it not for the fact that he drew blood from a couple of kids, it might have been humorous.

Soon after we purchased Mason, some friends came over; the primary purpose of the visit was to have their young kids see Mason. As the family came up the stairs, he did the lip thing and growled at each kid in turn. They pulled back their hands in fear and gingerly passed by the beast. When the dad's turn came, he didn't reel back but instead tried to actually pet the growling carnivore. When Mason bit the dad's finger, he was promptly hurled halfway across the room with the backside of a hand. While Mason pulls the lip routine to this day, he has warmed right up to the hand he bit, and the two now get along famously. This episode taught me that you need to let the dog know who is boss right from the start, a philosophy I adopted from that moment forward.

It's funny to see people react to an eight-pound creature lashing out. Why a person with a 20-to-1 advantage in size and weight is afraid of the growl-and-lip routine is beyond me, but most people quickly pull back. I think it's the intimidating lip more than anything else. There are some exceptions, and these people, like me, will simply kick a boisterous ankle-high dog out of the way when it is threatening them. But the majority of people back off, utterly intimidated by what this little pile of fur might do to them. Watching adults cower when Mason bares his teeth is quite comical, and my initial anger at Mason's behavior has become a combination of respect for his tenacity and pity for people's cowardice. When the kids bring friends home, it can be downright hilarious. I have witnessed a group of a half-dozen kids around the lip-wielding dog. Five of them nearly get their hands bitten off by even looking at him, and the sixth can reach over, pet him, and have him roll over for the full-body rubdown. Why I'll never know, but Mason actually warms to the occasional person for absolutely no discernible reason. All others beware.

I am embarrassed at having a dog that wants to nip at the nicest of people, especially children. What sort of a pet curls the lip and nips at cute neighbor kids who only want to pet him? When guests arrive at our home, we actually have to tell them not to pet the dog or he might bite them. That's an inviting greeting: "Hi. Welcome to our home. This is our dog, Mason. He's cute, but don't touch him or he'll bite you." I think I'm going to regret the fact that I don't have specific liability insurance for dog-biting.

In addition to generally hating most people, Mason showed a penchant for barking from the moment he arrived. Now, I'm okay with a dog barking when there is a purpose. Alerting us to burglars, for example, would be an excellent occasion to bark. Moreover, if the house were burning, I would certainly welcome the dog barking to wake us up and alert us to impending death. You know, like those personal drama stories you read about in *Reader's Digest* where the dog saves an entire family, sometimes sacrificing its own life in the process.

I also give the dog a pass if it yips when someone steps on it or sets a chair leg on its tail, which has happened on numerous occasions at our house. From the beginning, however, Mason didn't have the foggiest idea of when he should bark and when he should not bark. He simply barks all the time. Sometimes I think he barks because he's bored, or maybe just because he knows it bugs me. He'll bark when people come to the door, of course, but he'll also bark at the door for no apparent reason. Perhaps he imagines that someone is there or is trying to anticipate when someone will be there. He'll occasionally go wandering through the house just barking for the sake of it, as if he has something important to say.

The thing I like least about Mason, or any dog for that matter, is the dragging-his-butt-across-the-carpet habit. He demonstrated this in his first days home, and it has been a regular part of his routine. I get it that dogs don't have fingers to scratch with, and I guess I can also see why the carpet would work pretty well as a scratching device. But it is still quite disgusting, and no matter how many times the carpet has been cleaned, I can't bring myself to lie on any spot where Mason has dragged his butt.

I have never seen a dog drag his butt across the yard, and only rarely have I seen him drag it across the pavement. The scratcher of choice is carpet, and it is always in the center of the room. I wonder what dogs did hundreds of years ago when there were no carpets. Clearly, the advent of technology and creature comforts has benefited dogs as well as humans.

The response from my family to the butt dragging is the same as that from most "dog lovers," and that is that it is expected and accepted behavior and should be tolerated, no questions asked. I have learned to adapt and try to minimize the impact on the carpet by shouting the familiar "Mason, *no!*" every time I see it happen. I also frequently have the carpet cleaned.

QUALITY-OF-LIFE ADJUSTMENT

When we purchased Chipper, I somehow knew that we were not in it for the long haul. At the time, I sensed that Chipper would be just another in a string of pets that experienced short life cycles at our home. I intuitively knew that he would go the way of Crystal, the snake; Gizmo, the hamster; and One, Two, Orange and White, the fish, and I was good with that. I assumed that he would be hit by a car or would run away, and while I never suspected that we would return him as defective merchandise, I was glad he was gone. (In an ironic turn of events, I now find myself occasionally longing for Chipper's return when I consider my current situation.)

With the purchase of Mason it was a different story. The investment alone was reason enough to hang on to this dog, not to mention all the hoops we went through to get him. As much as I wanted to live without him, I had both financial and emotional resources invested in this dog, and I expected a return on this investment. That return should rightfully be a tranquil home life with a quite, obedient dog that brings love and joy to the entire family. While it was clear from the start that Mason was going to need some work, I had every confidence that a combination of family love and discipline from me would straighten this dog out. There was going to be no quick fix for this purchase, and I knew I was going to have to settle in for a long-term lifestyle adjustment. However, the deal was done and I was prepared for the challenge. I also knew, based on the preliminary defects I observed in this dog that it was not going to be a step up in my life. But by carefully and creatively working on the dog's behavior, I was confident that I could reach a point of tolerance that would allow me to get through having Mason in my home while keeping my sanity in check.

I could not believe the things we found ourselves doing in bringing this dog into our lives. Our entire home life changed in order to accommodate him, and it all happened so suddenly. We got the dog because we thought he would bring joy to the family, but instead he entirely disrupted the great circle of life within our home. My plan to tailor his behavior fell apart before it started.

To start with, there was the feeding. You may not know this, but dogs are not the sharpest knives in the drawer, and most dogs would die if you forgot to feed them; Callie, of course, being the self-sufficient and rare exception. Unlike babies, they don't cry when they're hungry. They don't even bark when there is no food (which I would consider acceptable behavior when starving). Unlike cats, they don't fend for themselves but are completely dependent on someone caring for them. It's amazing that dogs ever made it in the wild prior to being domesticated. One of the things I like about cats—although I've never owned one—is that they can kill their own food, which is pretty handy. Even if you never feed a pet cat, he will be fine because he's self-sufficient, and I have to respect that.

A cat is smart enough not to starve to death, whereas a dog doesn't have the foggiest idea how to make it in life without you. A cat doesn't need you, but simply allows you to own it. Cats are manly. But a dog would never survive in the house, let alone in the wild, without people.

With the arrival of a new puppy, it was sort of a given that we couldn't count on the kids to feed him, or he would most certainly die; the kids barely remember to feed themselves. No, the burden of keeping the dog alive fell upon us, which in our case meant my wife, since I made it clear from the moment the dog arrived that I was going to have nothing to do with feeding or in any other way supporting him. It was part of our "dog prenuptial agreement," in which I negotiated a quite favorable deal for myself. I agreed to allow the dog in my house in exchange for doing *nothing* to care for him. From now on there would be a required morning and evening feeding, just one more item of daily life that my poor wife was required to endure. She gets sole credit for getting Mason from puppy to adult; because if it had been left to the kids, he wouldn't have had food or water past the second week.

Then there is the matter of letting the dog out. Once again, cats are way out in front on this one. Even if you didn't have a litter box, I'm quite sure you'd never know when or where a cat "did his thing." Most cats are discreet and proper and have earned the privilege of living in the house. But dogs have to be let out, and if it's not on their time schedule, then you can just plan on paying the consequences: a yellow stain on the carpet or a log or two in the corner. There is absolutely no appreciation on the part of the dog for the privilege of living in the house, much like a teenager. Once you're in the family, you have a permanent seat, regardless of how much you may trash the place.

To this day Mason has never quite gotten the peeing-outside concept figured out, and since he was a puppy, it's been hit or miss—quite literally—on whether he could hold it until we let him outside. Our entire daily schedule had to revolve around when someone could let him out, and schedules were planned around who was available to take care of Mason during our absence. If we had to rely on the kids, we could just plan to haul out the paper towels and bleach (which to this day is a regular occurrence anyway). To ask the neighbors to help was quite bold, since they risked getting bitten every time they opened the door to let him outside. I think they also understood Mason's defecation potential, having seen the evidence quite frequently on their lawns.

ODD TRAITS

Like all creatures, Mason has his own set of individual characteristics that set him apart. I could probably list pages of them, but in order to focus on those traits unique to Mason and not to the dog world in general, I'll highlight only a few.

I've already referenced the strange way in which he holds his lip. It is funny, but it's also a bit unsettling. Every time he does the lip routine, you get the feeling that he is not playing with a full deck. Having a deranged dog can be a fearful thing, especially when you've been through what I've been through with dogs. You never know what Mason is thinking, but when he does the lip thing, it doesn't look as if *he* knows what he's thinking, and that is worse.

If the lip routine were symmetrical, Mason would probably look fierce and threatening, perhaps like an angry wolf. However, only one side of the lip is drawn back, because it gets caught behind one of his incisors, while the other side stays normal. Rather than looking fierce, he conveys a "duh" look, the kind of look he might have if he'd just polished off a six-pack. It isn't scary enough to back you off, yet it is abnormal enough to cause you to look the other way.

Another physical defect in this supposedly perfect dog is his blinking aberration. Put simply, he does not blink. At first you don't notice it because, of course, there is never any real reason to look at the dog for more than a moment, especially when lip is caught behind tooth. But if you get into a stare-down with Mason, you will find that he does not blink. Ever. His eyes don't water, he doesn't flinch or otherwise move; he simply stares blankly at you. It's unsettling. It's hard to tell whether he's staring at you or instead has expired mid-stare and rigor mortis has set in.

I again attribute the lack of blinking as evidence of the lack of anything going on in his head. When you get the combination of the lip and the blinkless stare, it is like looking into the eyes of a stuffed animal. Frankly, I would prefer him as a mantel ornament.

Mantel ornament: November calendar photo

Another weird thing Mason does is shake when he is excited or nervous. Anytime he gets in the car or boat he shakes uncontrollably. It's hard to say whether the cause is nerves or fear, but the shaking is fierce and frantic. On occasion, he will join us for a walk on a nearby nature trail. As we drive there in the car, he sits on my wife's lap next to the open window. He shakes so violently that she has to hold him tightly so that he doesn't jump or fall out the window. I often hold my wife's hand during these drives and otherwise distract her while at the same time jerking the car sharply "to avoid hitting a squirrel," hoping Mason might accidentally fall out of the car. No such luck yet.

Mason can't pee under pressure. If you let him out on his own, he'll be back at the door in moments, having done his thing. If you go out with him, however, he'll wander from tree to tree, trying in vain to do his thing while staring at you in the process. When nothing happens he moves on to the next tree, hoping for better results. There is a big difference between "letting" him out and "taking" him out... like about fifteen minutes.

Our back deck leads to some stairs, which Mason must go down in order to reach the lawn. (For some reason he will pee only on grass or carpet, not on the deck.) At times he is so excited to get outside and go, he can't find his way down the stairs. He prances around the deck and needs to be led to the stairs and given a nudge to get him to the grass.

Another Mason trait is his look of guilt when he's doing something wrong. The moment he bites someone, he knows he's in trouble and expects the punishment. His face shows guilt the instant he misbehaves. This is especially evident when he is left home alone with access to the full house. If he is lying in his bed by the door with his eyes open staring at you when you get home, then you know that there is a pile of poop or pee that needs to be dealt with somewhere in the house. His unblinking eyes give it away.

ORIFICE OVERLOAD

We have owned Mason for about eight years now, and since the day he arrived in our home, he has always used his orifices without hesitation. He really doesn't seem to have a preference; any orifice will do, as long as something comes out of it. To my knowledge, his ears are the only holes that have not delivered some form of liquid onto my carpet, and I can't even be sure of that.

At our house we refer to it as the "Three Ps": Peeing, Pooping, and Puking. Mason delivers each of the Three Ps very well and has been known to deliver all three simultaneously, although this can't be confirmed by an objective observer. I don't recall the subject of simultaneous orifice flow being brought up at the placement interview. If it had, I most certainly would have ordered a dog without any Ps, let alone three. Frankly, I feel that I was a bait-and-switch victim. There should be a lemon law for dogs, and were it not that we have passed the seven-year statute of limitations,

I might very well take legal action against somebody for misrepresentation.

From the start, Mason exhibited his ability to use bodily fluids in nondescript ways. We learned early during the Chipper Affair that the proper way to train a puppy was to put him in a small cage where there was no room to poop or pee. Puppies supposedly have a natural tendency to want to avoid contact with their bodily fluids. It seemed to work well with Chipper, since he never had the 3P problem, at least in the house. His biggest difficulty was simply the sheer size of his events as they accumulated on the lawn. We immediately purchased a small cage for Mason to sleep in, in order to train him early.

If the idea of "going" outside had worked with Mason, we really wouldn't have had a problem. He would have to pee for a year to discharge the amount Chipper did in one sitting, and there would not have been any noticeable lawn damage. I couldn't care less where the dog goes outdoors as long as it doesn't mess with my lawn. Unfortunately, it's a tossup as to whether Mason pees more indoors or out.

Mason apparently didn't inherit the gene that makes puppies averse to bodily fluids, since after the first night he was covered head to toe in everything he could possibly conjure from his body. And it wasn't as if he accidentally got some on him. It was as if he took great pleasure in rolling in it, because that would be the only explanation for how extensively he was covered. Worse, he looked happy when he came out of the cage, and it wasn't an "I'm happy to see you" sort of happy; it was a "What a great day to be alive" sort of happy. Odd, considering the condition he was in.

Thinking that this might have been an aberration or uncontrolled response to his first night away from his mom, we tried again. The second night was no different. Mason had another romp in the poop, seemingly to his satisfaction. On subsequent nights we alternated strategies, sometimes placing him in the closet with some newspaper, other times making sure he didn't have anything to eat or drink in the previous twenty-three hours. He never fully learned the art of "holding it," but in time and with age things did improve to the point where it was not an every-night occurrence, although that was even worse. It became hit or miss, pardon the pun, and it was frustrating not knowing under what basis he was going to have a steady flow of accidents during the night. Since I was the first one up in the morning, I would be the first to learn what sort of a night Mason had had. I would reluctantly turn on the light, afraid of what I would find.

At a very early age, it became clear that Mason was the Houdini of the dog world. Whether keeping him in a closet or behind a gate or a barricaded entryway, Mason always found a way out, over, under, or through. We've seen him unhook latches, work his way through self-closing doors, and slip under adjustable gates. While staying at my brother-in-law's house while we were on vacation (what was he thinking?), Mason escaped through a 2 x 4—and bar stool—barricaded structure that would have kept most *people* out. Once broken free from the kitchen, he proceeded to puke and pee on the carpet, thereby insuring that his first stay at the in-laws' would be his last. I never felt that bad about it because they went into dog sitting with eyes wide open. They were fully aware of Mason's shortcomings, yet they felt it would be fun. They learned.

The good news is that it gave my sister-in-law the excuse she needed to redecorate. A night of Mason unplugged is like a drunk out on a binge, and any sane person would seriously consider a major decorating makeover simply knowing what the poor floors had been through after a night of Mason.

A couple of years after what I now refer to as the "lemon purchase," we decided to move. Our new home required some minor decorating, and we proceeded to install new carpet, fresh paint, and a few pieces of new furniture. Before officially moving in, I installed a gate for Mason, knowing that I would be re-decorating very soon if I didn't.

It was not an elaborate gate, but it had a self-closing spring on the hinge, which forced the gate closed at all times. A couple of nights after we moved in, we found Mason sleeping in the basement. He had figured out a way to work the gate open with his nose or paw and make his way out. Any two-year-old could have done it, and I should have known to make the system a bit more robust. I modified the gate by installing one of those hook-and-eye latches. My wife can barely open one of those, so there was no way Mason could do it.

Within a couple of nights, however, we began to find Mason comfortably sleeping in the living room the next morning. How he opened the latch I do not know, but since it happened on more than one occasion, and knowing there was no secret Mason advocate lurking in the house during the night, I know he figured that one out as well.

So I moved the latch higher, thinking that having to stand on his hind feet to work the mechanism would simply be too much even for Mason. Besides, he wasn't tall enough to reach the latch; I made sure of that. Before too many nights went by, however, I found him wandering around the kitchen one morning, the gate fully locked and untouched. The only explanation was that he had climbed over the gate, and sure enough, a few nights later I heard a noise coming from the entryway. I sneaked out, peered through the kitchen, and saw Mason belly straddling the gate, having jumped up and pulled himself over. I watched, dumbfounded, as he hung suspended midsection over the top of the gate for a very long time. Whether he was just regaining his stamina or decided to take a short nap, I'm not sure, but there he was, looking like a sock hanging on a clothesline. It had to have been painful, but obviously it was worth the pain to Mason.

That was it. I was tired of the challenge and sick of the failures. The dog, while not smart, clearly had a penchant for working his way out of captivity. I built a new plywood gate, high enough that Mason couldn't have pole-vaulted his way over, and I then secured it with a mechanism that was up high and double-latched so that only two hands could open it. That finally solved the problem.

A very unfortunate incident led to the ultimate gate solution and at the same time, forever altered my already shaking relationship with Mason. After we had been in the new house for only a few months, Mason had a romp through the house one night that almost sealed his doom. The next morning, when I entered the kitchen while it was still dark, I glanced toward the living room and saw what appeared to be large black spots, about four inches in diameter, dotting the beige carpet. At first, I thought they were shadows from something outdoors that were magnified in the bright moonlight. Upon closer observation, it looked as if someone had laid a giant Twister board in the living room, black circles on a light background silhouetted by the moonlight shining through the skylights. Not wanting to be abducted by an alien if in fact something extraterrestrial was going on, I cautiously walked into the room and quickly flipped on a light switch.

With the lights on, it was instantly apparent that this was not the work of an intelligent life form or even a prankster. These puddles were clearly the result of dog barf that could be the work of only one artist. Remembering the as yet unsolved gate problem, I immediately looked for Mason, who I found lying on the couch with one of those "Yes I did it and I'm really sorry" looks on his face. Grabbing the dog, I shoved his face into every puddle of barf I could find and yelled the customary "Bad Dog!" at him after each face-in-the-barf thrust, which was many times because there were many puddles of barf. It was amazing that so much puke (the third P) could come out of such a small creature. (I don't believe the term "Bad Dog!" has ever effectively been used to correct bad dog behavior, but it certainly makes the dog owner feel better by saying it, especially when it is said with added emphasis on *bad*.)

As I carried him back to the entryway from which he'd escaped, I noticed more puddles in the den, every bit as numerous as those in the living room. When putting—more like throwing—Mason back into the entryway, I noticed one of the kids' backpacks torn open and candy wrappers of all sorts strewn about. I had heard that chocolate kills dogs, but I couldn't be so lucky. Mason must have eaten a pound of chocolate and most of the accompanying wrappers, but instead of dying, he decided to puke the semi-digested chocolate onto the carpet. The new carpet. The new carpet that was only in two rooms. The new carpet that was separated by a huge tiled kitchen floor and several hallways with old carpet. Here was a house full of tile and old carpet, but he chose to ruin only the new carpet that was just in two rooms. It was probably this single event that most influenced our future relationship.

GOING NAUTICAL

I will give Mason credit for one thing: it doesn't take much to please him. Two things that especially bring him enjoyment—if you don't count upsetting me—are chasing tennis balls and riding in a boat. I will discuss the tennis ball issue later, and you will soon see that he is basically unsuited for riding in a boat.

We live on a lake and therefore take frequent rides in our speedboat. These are typically slow-paced events where we putt along and enjoy the sights and sounds. Mason has developed quite a liking for boat rides; he goes nuts when he has the opportunity to join us for a ride on the boat.

The standard line is *"Masonwannagoforaboatride?!"*—which must be said with an excited expression and preferably within inches of his face. When he hears this high-pitched question, his face lights up, he starts bouncing up and down as if his legs are pogo-sticks; he's beside himself with excitement and can barely contain himself. (Just for sheer fun, a couple of times each winter I'll get in his face and shout

"*Masonwannagoforaboatride?!*" In the dark of a Michigan winter, you do what you can to bring some joy and excitement to the day, and that always does it.)

Mason on a boat ride

As we head to the boat after the announcement, Mason prances down the dock, occasionally looking back at the family as if in disbelief that this could really be happening to him. Each time he treats it as if it is the best thing that ever happened in his little doggie life, testifying once again to the smallness of a dog's world.

From the moment he gets onboard until we get back, he runs back and forth repeatedly from bow to stern. He runs to the bow, strains his neck over the railing as if taking a nautical bearing and then dashes to the stern as if to get one last look at where we've been. He does this for two hours straight, seemingly unable to control himself. It's exhausting to watch.

Of course, what outing with Mason would be complete without his favorite pastime, which would be delivering one of the 3Ps? It is as if the perfect storm of excitement, nerves, and "I'm going to stick it to the man" attitude converge when Mason gets on the boat, because he delivers each P in succession on one out of two outings.

After his initial reconnaissance run, he will pee, poop, and/or puke uncontrollably and often in succession when he's going nautical. On the boat, he isn't even discreet about it, often dropping a load right on the front seat cushion or lifting a leg in front of everyone as he drains all over the carpet. Discipline and anger are pointless, since he's like a dog possessed. I feel sorry for the poor swimmer who bumps into a floating dog turd, but the reality is that there is only one venue for a misplaced dog-log, and that is over the side. I tell myself that the fish will eat it.

There have been numerous opportunities to rid myself of Mason on these boat trips. Perhaps an accidental drowning or losing him in the dunes while hiking on shore. The problem is that everyone is in close proximity on a boat outing, and creating an "accident" in stealth is a bit tricky with the wife and kids around.

We came close to losing Mason on one occasion, and it had nothing to do with me and everything to do with Mason. I could only have hoped for events to come to their inevitable conclusion, but like the Phoenix, Mason rose from the grip of the sea. It was early spring, when the water on Lake Michigan is still ice cold. Hypothermia would set in and kill any human, but as I've learned since owning Mason, dogs can be quite resilient to things that might take out a man. We were out on the boat one evening. The water was flat and we were a couple of miles from shore, just cruising along enjoying the sights.

As we headed toward our favorite dune and began to turn toward shore, someone yelled out that Mason was gone. Feigning concern, I pulled back on the throttle to assess the situation. Sure enough, no Mason. *Oh well*, I thought, *it sucks to be him.* As I pretended to do something—while contemplating a pleasant life without Mason—someone spotted a boat approaching from behind. As it drew closer, we heard the horn blaring and saw the people gesturing toward the shore. There, as a barely visible bobbing white dot in the water, was Mason doggy paddling toward shore, a mile or more away.

I may have failed to mention that Mason likes to swim. Every time he spots the dunes, he will do all he can to get to them, even if it involves swimming. Apparently, the lure of the dunes on the horizon was more than he could stand, since he obviously jumped overboard and began swimming to shore, thinking he'd get there on his own before we would by boat.

Almost lost in open water!

It was too good to be true: two miles from shore, forty-five degree water, and nobody paying attention when the dog jumps overboard. Unfortunately, I had a boat full of Mason lovers screaming in fear for his life. We turned the boat around and headed back to save the pooch. I tried to steer into the dog but missed, and before I could make another attempt, my youngest dived into the frigid water to save Mason. Now I truly had a stake in the rescue operation, so made every attempt to assist. The dog I could easily do without but not the boy. Both boy and dog made it safely back into the boat, and neither appeared negatively affected by the experience.

Here was the perfect scenario for losing the dog, and yet by the will of God *or the curse of the devil*, Mason survived another day to torment me. The dog has more lives than a cat, and once again, the opportunity for a better life was lost. What if we had been another mile out; would the other boat have seen Mason jump overboard? What if I had been going faster; might the other boat never have caught up with us? What if a great white shark had worked its way into Lake Michigan and mistaken Mason for a misplaced baby seal? Unfortunately, there is no use in reliving the past. It is what it is, and I can only look toward tomorrow, hoping for a better outcome for future events.

Mason boating with my son

ON A WALK

———oOo— 🦴 —oOo———

Most people take their dogs for walks, but have you ever noticed how few of them are really taking the *dog* for a walk? Most often it is the other way around, with the dog owner oblivious to the irony, let alone the comical display of perceived control. Since the leash is around the dog's neck, one assumes that the person is in charge. In reality, however, the dog is fully aware of who is pulling this cart and is perfectly content to tow the load while leaving his passenger with ego intact.

As I have said previously, Callie the Collie would simply not go on a walk. It wasn't that he was averse to the leash; he just refused to leave the property, which made me love him even more. He was truly maintenance free in that he refused to be maintained. How I long for a dog like Callie. In fact, I've often longed for my kids to be like Callie.

Mason, on the other hand and true to form, bucks the typical dog trend when it comes to walks. He will go for a walk but reluctantly and only on his own terms. The problem is you never know what his *terms* will be. All you know for sure is that at some point he will have had enough. He will willingly go on the walk and sometimes even feign joy in doing so. He'll do the head bob, bounce up and down once or twice, twirl around, and sometimes teasingly throw out a bark. Don't be deceived, however; it's all theatrics.

We have miles of very nice bike paths in our town, which are ideal for walks, with or without dogs (or people) in tow. Additionally, there are beautifully groomed lawns on either side of the bike paths, suitable for softer walking or, if you're a dog, pooping.

It's within the context of these parameters that you must envision Mason "walking." Beautiful day, maintained paths, groomed lawns—everything a dog could want. Now picture a husband and wife out for a leisurely stroll, taking the dog along for some exercise and companionship. (Of course, don't imagine me in this setting, as I would never voluntarily do anything pleasurable with Mason—or with any other dog, for that matter—since that would be, as they say, a paradox.)

You also must picture Mason on the leash, but unlike any other normal dog in the universe, Mason does not lead; he follows. At first blush, this may seem like a good thing, since the dog apparently recognizes his place: a follower, not a leader. The reason, however, is not that he is deferring to his more intelligent mammal brethren but rather that he is just plain lazy.

It usually happens mid-walk, but sometimes as early as two or three hundred yards down the path. It starts with us merrily walking along when all of a sudden the leash draws taut. Mason freezes in place and my wife—who is holding the leash since I don't have to because of the dog prenup—is brought to a sudden stop. When this happens, either the leash falls out of her hand because she was holding it too loosely, or she was holding on too tightly and the sudden stop pulls her off balance. In either case, these would be among the few times you would hear my wife let out an expletive, both well timed and very appropriate.

Out for a walk: July calendar photo

Mason, for inexplicable reasons, decides he's had enough and simply stops. As I've said, it may be mere minutes into the walk. It's not that he tires, slows down, and indicates that he's getting ready to go home. He just stops dead in his tracks, which is what he'd be if I were holding the leash. He truly thinks he's calling the shots and thinks that by stopping we'll pick him up and carry him home. This is what happened the first few times because my wife has a soft heart, but even she has her limits.

Walks on a leash came to an end because there really wasn't any walking involved on the part of the dog. In the final days before we stopped taking Mason on walks, she would literally drag him until he decided to start walking again. I would cheer her on, since seeing Mason's butt being dragged on the paved bike path was sweet revenge for all the times he's dragged it across my living room carpet.

We have tried taking Mason on walks on some dune trails near our home. Of course he likes the freedom and generally stays near us. It still is a chore, however, because due to either attitude or physical limitations, he just won't keep up. We call and coax, but Mason will follow along at his own pace, not caring that he is holding up our walk. All the other people walking dogs either have the dog obediently and properly walking with the leash or running ahead as a decent dog should do. But again, Mason is anything but decent or normal and can't even do a walk properly.

Since we are bigger than dogs and allegedly much further along in the evolutionary process, we are in charge, and that dog is going to do whatever we say it will do; it's that simple. Better than watching the dog being dragged behind a leash, however, is not having to take him on walks at all. Since Mason was banished for life from walks, I truly enjoy our walks again and don't miss having Mason in tow one bit. In fact, I feel a sense of accomplishment every time I see people walk by in tow behind their dogs. I feel superior that I've figured out how to tame and master the savage beast while "man's best friend" is still dragging so many others on miserable walks. Life is *so* much more enjoyable not having to pretend that I'm enjoying walking the dog.

THE MASON CALENDAR

I think most people have a sinister side that gives them pleasure when they annoy others. Children frequently demonstrate this annoyance technique, as when their intentional annoyance generates the "Don't touch me!" response. This leads to a further "touch" which leads to hitting which results in full-fledged fighting, the intended purpose of the original touch. My wife comes from a family with five girls. She tells of the time when she was a child and her older sister would pin her down on the floor by sitting on her. She would then let the saliva hang down over my wife's face to its breaking point, then slurp it back before it would break away. That is an example of an annoyance, and a pretty good one at that. Human nature derives a certain satisfaction by finding and then pushing the buttons that upset and annoy other people.

As adults, our annoyance tendencies are a bit more subtle, and, while they rarely lead to blows, they have a certain satisfying quality nonetheless. Nowhere do people rub each other the wrong way more than in families, especially as they get older. In any given family, members know what bugs each other, and invariably a family reunion or other gathering results in one member's idiosyncrasy being exploited by another for the sole purpose of enjoyment. It is part of the redeeming quality of the family unit, and those who don't recognize this fact miss out on one of life's simple pleasures. Simply put, teasing is fun.

There is a particular person in my extended family who is a bit of a prankster and takes pleasure in teasing. This particular person—who will be unnamed to protect her identity—has an unusual affection for dogs, which, as you might expect, would put her at odds with me on the subject. This affection for dogs goes far beyond what is normal and is what makes my own form of teasing particularly gratifying to me.

Most people—I am admittedly the exception—love their pets, but there are those people who love their pets beyond the bounds of normalcy. This is especially evident in excessive dog lovers, the people who not only love their dogs as much as their own children; they truly *consider* them children. I call them "beyond-reason dog lovers." Beyond-reason dog lovers talk endlessly about something their dog just did, as if you care, much the way new parents talk about how their baby just rolled over for the first time, about which you do care. These people don't think twice about bringing their dog along when invited to your home for a visit. The thought of having their shedding, drooling, butt-dragging, smelly, barking rodent of a dog waltz through your living room, leaving behind a pile of poop, piddle of pee, or patch of puke when it leaves, doesn't bother them in the least. In fact, the offense of it doesn't even cross their minds.

The beyond-reason dog lover thinks nothing of dropping one thousand dollars for some pointless surgery on their beagle, yet forgets the annual dental checkup for their child. I particularly like the person who is in tears because poor Fido has "cancer," as if they can detect it, let alone treat it in a dog.

Doctor: "Mrs. Jones, your dog has cancer. I recommend we perform immediate surgery, followed by a heavy dose of radiation and subsequent chemotherapy treatments."

Mrs. Jones: "Oh doctor, of course we'll do it. Anything to keep my Fido alive."

Of course, Fido is already ten-years-old and ready to keel over anyway from old age, but it's only money.

Now that you know what I really think about beyond-reason dog lovers, and now that you know there is at least one in my family, you can appreciate the extent to which my exploitation of this love-of-dog idiosyncrasy gave me such enjoyment. Anything for a good laugh.

It was at a family Christmas party several years ago when the thought came to me, probably in an eggnog-induced state. My wife had famously made Christmas calendars each year, affixing the photo of a grandchild to each month and giving the calendar to the grandparents and siblings as a constant reminder throughout the year of each grandchild in the family. These calendars were a hit, and everyone waited with eager anticipation to receive their calendars each Christmas.

One Christmas, while watching everyone ogle over the calendars, it occurred to me how much fun it would be to put a pet on the calendar but with a twist. Rather than have the pet on the calendar as a reminder of how cute and cuddly it was, why not put the pet on the calendar in the most derogatory and insulting way possible, offending anyone who was a beyond-reason dog lover? This would be the mother of all insults, one that would actually offend several people in the family and our extended circles. (Why waste a good insult on just your family? I could distribute the calendar to several people who we thought could use a good laugh and maximize our efforts.)

Of course, in our family, it was only one person who would truly get genuinely upset by such a calendar. Knowing how much she knows I hate Mason, it would arouse added ire to use my *beloved* Mason as the subject of the calendar. Rather than a Playmate of the Month, there would be a Mason of the Month, and instead of scantily dressed, I would photograph Mason in various humiliating settings, intended solely to anger the beyond reason dog-loving crowd. At the end of the year we would print the calendars using the photos and then hand them out at Christmas. This calendar would be the perfect gift that keeps on giving. I could envision the look of shock and anger on her face a year in advance, and it brought me joy just contemplating it.

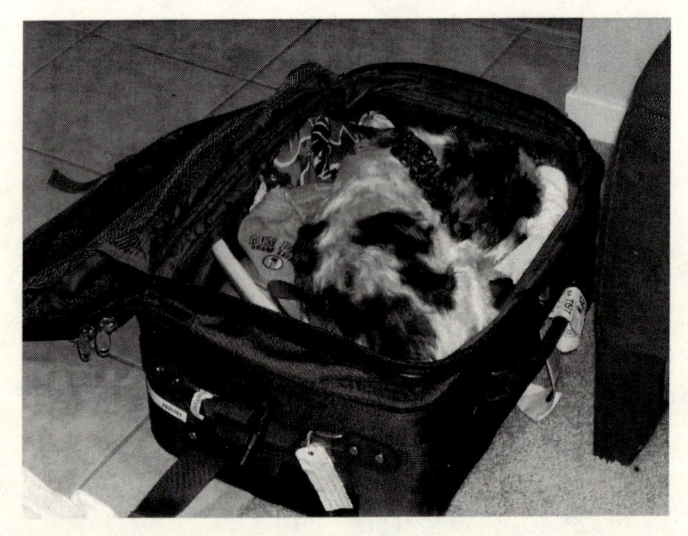

One-way trip: January calendar photo

We needed twelve high-quality photos, we being me and my accomplices—my wife and son—both of whom quickly latched onto the idea, wanting to enjoy some of the sadistic pleasure the project would provide. (While they don't share my distaste for Mason, their love of a good laugh trumped any hesitation they might have had.) Thinking up settings and poses for Mason that would be the most offensive to the beyond-reason dog lover made me break out in goose bumps of joy. I imagined it being akin to the feeling experienced by the guy who once wrote the book about one hundred uses for a dead cat. We considered any photo idea as long as it was offensive. My particular favorite was the one in which Mason had a rope tied around his neck with a brick tied to the other end. He was sitting at the end of the dock for this shot, which was my son's idea. I'm so proud of him. My son's favorite was when I put Mason on a rope and tied him to the bumper of my car. This was really a father-son bonding exercise.

More salt, please: February calendar photo

As is inevitable when the wife gets involved, we had the syrupy, cutesy shots as well. These included Mason peering out from a Halloween pumpkin, which unfortunately made it into the calendar as "Mason October." Fortunately, the shot of Mason as a Christmas decoration had to be eliminated since it was too cute and didn't meet the high offensive standards that had been established; we had to draw the line somewhere. Essentially, if the picture elicited a response like "Oh, he's so cute" or "That's darling," it was cut. If it was on the edge and questionable, it was included.

Drip-drying: March calendar photo

Naturally, the shots are offensive to the normal dog lover, which is the whole point, so imagine how offensive they were to the beyond-reason dog lover! It was a remarkable sight and brought tears of laughter and joy to my eyes when she opened her calendar. All she could muster was "Uh-uh!"—sister-in-law-speak for "I can't believe you did this and you have got to be kidding you big loser of a dog-hating brother-in-law, you,"—as she looked at me with daggers coming from her eyes. The most gratifying part of offending a beyond-reason dog lover is that they genuinely think you're serious, which underscores a twisted sense of reality when it comes to dogs.

Had the calendar contained offensive pictures of her own dogs, I would have been dead where I was standing, and frankly, it might have been worth it. As it was, there was the perfect combination of offense, humor, and love, since only love could compel someone to take the time to create such a gift, and that's what I am about.

Finally being useful: April calendar photo

I'm not normally that sentimental, but I love my sister-in-law very much, and to see her bothered by something to this extent made me love her all the more. She would never admit it, but I know the feeling was mutual, and to this day

I believe she secretly considers me to be her favorite brother-in-law.

The calendar was a true hit, at least with the masses, creating a bit of a cult following within the extended-family-and-friends network. While not a die-hard Elvis fan, I think it would be similar to the bond created by those who collect velvet paintings of The King. While people, even non-family members, requested additional copies, we never reprinted the 2005 Mason Calendar. It is a limited-edition work of art, which will only grow in value and appeal in the years ahead. It was truly a labor of love and was the gift that kept on giving, and I am proud of it.

Return to sender: May calendar photo

Finally clean: August calendar photo

Hung over: September calendar photo

A woman's touch: October calendar photo

Merry Christmas: December calendar photo

VACATIONS

One of the great developments in the dog world over the years is dog boarding. Imagine what a world it would be if we had to take our dogs wherever we went. Some people love to take their dogs with them on vacations, which is why I shied away from camping early on. It's bad enough listening to a dog bark down the block from my home, but it's merciless to hear one through the canvas walls of a tent.

Whenever we go on vacation, my wife goes through a pre-vacation guilt trip about taking Mason to the dog boarding house. She thinks that Mason will get DBDS (Dog Boarding Distress Syndrome) simply by being in close proximity with a few dozen other dogs. Mason spends ninety-eight percent of his days at home lying on his rug in the corner of the room, so I can't imagine why it would be much different at the boarding house. Besides, I would expect him to enjoy hanging out exclusively with his own kind for a week or two. It might give him a new perspective on how good he really has it at our house.

My wife may be on to something, however, since even the vet in charge of the dog boarding house suspects Mason has some problems. On his most recent visit, Mason was away from home for all of one week. When we returned, the vet informed my wife that Mason spent the week pooping and peeing in his pen, which isn't surprising knowing Mason's history. As you know, the 3Ps is the same battle he has fought since being a pup, and he never truly grew out of it. If I wanted to describe the problem in modern medical parlance, I would call it TPNSD (Three Ps Neurological Stress Disorder). With my luck, now that it's named they'll come up with a pill that will solve the problem... right after Mason dies of old age.

Apparently, for the entire week Mason did his business in the pen and refused to do so on his daily walks with the vet. I can empathize with the vet: *been there. Feel my pain.* As a result, we were asked not to bring him back to the boarding house, likely making him the first dog ever kicked out of a veterinary office. We were now left with a new dilemma in dog ownership: what to do with the dog when we go away.

I don't believe the word has spread, so I suspect we have a couple more vacations ahead of us since there are, I believe, two more dog boarding houses in the area. After that, however, we have a problem, since even our neighbors hate Mason and will likely not react well to being asked to watch him in our absence. The one time our neighbor agreed to watch him, Mason wouldn't go back in the house, so she had to pick him up and carry him in. Two days later, she had the worst case of poison oak I have ever seen in my life. Poor girl. One of the great ironies that have become my life would be that I could no longer take a vacation because I can't leave the very thing that in large part makes me need a vacation in the first place.

The worse scenario, however, is not the family vacation, but the one in which my wife leaves for her annual visit to see her father in Florida. I swear—and I literally do—that Mason intentionally defecates around the house when he wants to make me mad, which is what happened on my wife's last weekend away. She says it happened because he was mad that she left, but whatever the reason, he came within one poop of the proverbial long ride in the country.

The first day she was gone I made it a point of letting the dog out every couple of hours. In fact, I'd let him out through the front door, knowing he'd have to wander to the back door, his normal point of ingress and egress. Along the trek back he was bound to have ample opportunity to do any one of the Three Ps, assuring me of no cleanup in the house. It's important to strategize with an animal, to get into their head, so to speak. Or so I thought.

At bedtime, I allowed him one more walk outside and then locked him in the entryway. The next morning, as one might expect from a deranged dog, there was poop, pee, and puke all over the entryway. The Three Ps on full display and in ample abundance. Mason wasn't sick before he went to bed, and he hadn't ingested an abnormal amount of solids or liquids. Still, he can deliver at will, regardless of circumstances, and deliver he did. It was unbelievable. Even the kids were stunned. Never before had a dog unloaded so much in so short a period of time as Mason did that night. I didn't know whether to be in shock or in awe, because both emotions were appropriate, so I simply went to work cleaning things up. A half hour and half gallon of bleach later, things were back to normal, at least for the moment.

During the entire weekend my wife was gone, Mason unloaded in the entryway in some fashion, although not to the extent of that first night. I still let him out occasionally, but not on a regular basis and certainly not if it was an inconvenience. It became clear that there was no reason to let him out; he was going to go where and when he wanted to, in spite of my efforts at controlling him. Whether he was mad because my wife was gone or just trying to piss me off, the result was the same: uncontrolled orifice pandemonium.

When my wife returned, the Three Ps stopped as suddenly as they had begun. I chalked the episode up to a learning experience and moved on. Not only have I given up on the dog, I've also given up on any attempt to do my part in caring for him, even in my wife's absence. All I can do now is pray that he dies before her next trip, since I would not be able to make it through another weekend like that.

HOW MUCH CAN A MAN TAKE?

I'm only one man, as Regis likes to say, and as such cannot be expected to have unlimited tolerance for everything, especially Mason. Even a superman like Regis wouldn't have the fortitude to stick it out with this dog. I've been patient beyond what could be expected of any man, but even I have my limits. There are ongoing infringements on my levels of tolerance, and at some point I'm going to snap.

I've already made clear my lack of understanding for those who spend big money on dog surgery and the like. There has to be a limit on how much to spend on a dog, even for the most ardent beyond-reason dog lover. If you're willing to spend one thousand dollars on dog surgery, would you spend two thousand? How about five thousand? Certainly not *ten thousand*! There is no limit on what you'll spend on people, but there has to be a spending limit on dogs. There is a point at which everyone knows a dog must go whether due to cost, suffering, or old age. Why else do people "put down" their dogs?

In determining my own limit on what I'll allow the family to spend on Mason, I first categorize the expense into either maintenance or survival. Maintenance includes shots, worm pills, and grooming, all of which indirectly benefit the family. Since we have the dog, I certainly don't want him to have worms. All of his other disgusting habits are bad enough without knowing that worms are crawling around his intestines (and getting into the carpet). Grooming, too, has its merits for the family. While there is that offensive couple of weeks of butt dragging immediately following the grooming, the upside is the full cleaning and disinfecting of both the dog and carpet that result. The cleaning of the teeth also supposedly helps the dog's breath, although my experience has been that dogs never have good breath.

Shots, of course, are necessary for the safety of both the family and any unfortunate visitor who Mason nips at. Mason has drawn blood, and the last thing we need is one of the neighbor kids getting rabies. These maintenance costs are excessive, of course, and it's a racket to some extent. Why is it, for example, that a dog no bigger than my head requires an hour of hair cutting at three times the cost of my own haircut? Why bother grooming, for that matter? We all know what the dog does the moment he gets home. It's about as pointless as folding underwear. Besides, sixty-five dollars on shots and pills once or twice a year adds up. In eight years we've already spent more on the dog than we paid for him. No one would put that kind of ongoing investment into his car after eight years.

Maintenance costs are a slow creep, adding up over the years without you realizing it. That is why it is particularly difficult to spot that point when maintenance costs turn into survival costs. You can suddenly be throwing good money away on keeping a dog alive that, frankly, has run its course. My own self-imposed limit is $125, and that number was determined from a purely economic perspective. Since $125 is the going rate for putting a dog to sleep, it makes no sense to spend more than that keeping an eight-year-old dog alive. I'm told most dogs live to be ten to twelve years old, making a dog of eight past his prime. To keep a dog alive at this point is quite possibly prolonging his misery and pain, and I want no part of that. I would sooner do the dog, and my wallet, a favor and put him down now.

To sum it up, the maintenance costs are to be expected, but you need to stop throwing good money after bad when the time has come. In Mason's case, that time is as near as the next $125 vet bill.

It can get a bit lonely being the only person in the home who does not like the dog. I'm the only one who laughs at my dog jokes and sees the humor in ignoring Mason. There is so much to enjoy and appreciate in hating your dog, and yet it is wasted on only me. While I get great pleasure in antagonizing and ignoring the dog, I am in it alone and gain only personal satisfaction from my antics.

Worse than that, it works both ways. Because I am the only dog hater in the house, the rest of the family tries desperately to get back at me, siding with Mason at my expense. They are largely unsuccessful simply because I have more material to work with and am by nature much better at intentionally bugging people. Still, they have landed on one particular act that genuinely causes me heartburn.

Every family has nicknames for members of the family, and these names are given as acts of love and affection in order to tighten the family bonds. This is all well and good. I firmly believe, however, that the line should be drawn when it comes to pets, and dogs in particular. Since a dog is not a member of the family by virtue of its genetic makeup, it has no rights to many family privileges, and that includes nicknames. Apparently my family didn't get the memo on this one.

How they got to this point, I don't know, but when my wife and kids talk to Mason, they refer to themselves in the third person.

My wife: "Mason, do you want your mommy to give you a bath?"

One of my sons: "Mason, come to your boy"

What really hurts, though, is when they pick him up, put him up to my face, and say, "Mason, do you want to go to your daddy?" First of all, I am not his daddy, and second of all, I am not his anything. I'm not his daddy, his master, or his owner. If I have to be referred to as his "something" then I am his nemesis.

Of course, this has now become a sadistic game since the family knows how much this bothers me. The best I can do is walk away when the daddy term comes up and wait for the moment to pass. It happens no less than twice a week, but I look at it from a pragmatic perspective. If this is the worse they can do to get back at me for not liking the dog, I'm not doing too bad.

THE TUMMY RUB

People do peculiar things with their pets, some of which are downright repulsive. Letting the dog lick your face would be one of the repugnant activities, knowing where that tongue has been during the day. The dog has licked the floor, his old chew toy, his own genitals, the garbage can, and likely the toilet, and now I'm going to let him lick my face? I don't think so.

And take shedding. Why do the same people who make you take your shoes off so you won't get dirt in their house think nothing about letting the dog, which rarely has its hair washed, run around the house dropping dirty hair everywhere it goes? Of course, we never had that problem with Mason, since one of the features we ordered for our dream dog was being shed-less. (It was also just about the only feature we ordered that was actually delivered.)

In our case, there are several things about Mason that are repulsive. I've already described in some detail the dog's own hygiene deficiencies, which manifest themselves on the carpets of our home. There is also the dirt he drags into the house. When I say "drag," that is exactly what I mean. Mason is so low to the ground and his hair so long that whatever he happens to walk through ends up in our home. If he walked through wet grass, he ends up drying himself on the carpet as he walks back into the house. If he walked through dirt, our furniture serves as a depository for the accumulated grime. The worst are the burrs he picks up from the underbrush. These invariably end up scratching whoever comes into contact with the dog, which of course does not affect me, since Mason and I make it a point never to touch.

The strangest interaction between the family and Mason is the tummy rub. Let me start by saying that I'd pay good money to get the kind of tummy rub that Mason gets. To be coddled, caressed, and ogled that way would be a dream come true for any man, but for some reason a woman will reach out and pet, scratch, rub, caress, and snuggle with a dog far more quickly than she will with any man. And yes, I have confirmed this to be the case with other men, lest you think it is something exclusive to me. All Mason has to do is walk over to my wife, casually lie on his back, and spread his legs to reveal his doghood with confident expectation. He is never disappointed because the rubbing of the tummy commences immediately, to the enjoyment of both dog and wife. I don't know whether to be disgusted or jealous.

I'm under no illusion in knowing that if I walked up to my wife and lay on my back spread-eagle expecting a tummy rub, I'd be slapped silly. Frankly, it's one of life's great injustices that a dog can get more physical attention than a man can. Besides, I think my underside is every bit as attractive and enticing as Mason's is.

And Mason doesn't always initiate the tummy rub. More often one of the family will make the first move and, as announcing a boat ride, say in one of those high-pitched dog-come-hither voices, "*Masonwannahaveatummyrub?!*" Of *course*, he does—who wouldn't—but he has learned to be casual about it, sauntering over and then dropping into a roll as if to say, "Okay, if you really want to do this..." Maybe that's my problem. Maybe if I play hard to get...

My wife administers the ultimate tummy rub. She picks up the dog, cradles him like a newborn, and then proceeds to give the tummy rub with one hand while cradling him with the other. As he lies there, head falling back over her arm, he gives what I swear is a "na-na-na-na-boo-boo" glance my way. He knows darn well that at that moment he has it better than I do and he's milking it for everything it's worth. What makes it worse is that she carries on a simultaneous conversation with me, absolutely oblivious to the irony. I have no doubt that it's his way of getting back at me for all the times I've avoided, kicked, yelled at, or otherwise lashed out at him. He savors every moment of it.

MORE LIVES THAN A CAT

I thought Mason had hit his $125 medical limit one day when I was working on the lawn. It was spring, and I was preparing the lawn with fertilizer. As I turned around to push the spreader back the way I had come, I noticed Mason doubled over on the other end of the lawn. After I got the mail, put the spreader away, had a sandwich and grabbed a phone call, I urgently made my way to him to see what was wrong. He was throwing up, and I could only assume—and secretly hope—that he had ingested some fertilizer. I think he probably did, but as luck would have it he survived to live another day.

Ready for a dip: June calendar photo

Another time we were backing out of the driveway when one of the kids, thinking he was under the car, screamed, "Look out for Mason!" I completed pulling out of the driveway, swerved back and forth to increase my odds, and then got out of the car, hoping that I'd see a furry outline of the dog on the pavement. Again, it was not to be, and Mason came trotting from around the side of the house, lip tucked neatly behind his incisor.

One Saturday I was working around the yard with Mason lounging in the driveway as I worked. I began to head into the house when I noticed him following me. He hesitated when he came to the entry step and gave what seemed to be a pained leap to make it up the stair. Once up, he stopped briefly, as if to gather his strength, before continuing into the house, treading gingerly. I thought that I might be witnessing the early stages of old age creeping up, and I grinned to myself thinking that surely the end must be soon. That evening my wife mentioned that she had taken Mason in for shots that day—four of them, which were causing him severe pain. I *knew* it was too good to be true.

Tennis anyone?

Mason never did well at the normal dog things. No one should assume that all dogs can catch a Frisbee in flight any more than all people can dunk a basketball. But in the same way that most people can actually pick up a basketball, one might assume that most dogs can fetch a ball. If *most* implies there are exceptions, then Mason is an exception, as he does not know how to fetch a ball.

At our house we have a basket full of old tennis balls. The game of fetch is supposed be played like this: Master picks up tennis ball; dog stands poised in the "I can't wait to get the tennis ball" position; master throws ball; dog races after ball, tackles it, and brings it back to master, dropping it dutifully at his feet. When the game is played properly, the dog does his best to retrieve the ball in a way that pleases his master.

A typical game of fetch with Mason goes like this: Reluctant master picks up tennis ball; Mason stands poised in the "I can't wait to bug him" position; reluctant master throws ball; dog races after ball, tackles it, plays with it for five minutes, casually walks back to master, dropping ball teasingly ten feet from reluctant master. Reluctant master tries to retrieve ball, only to have Mason run away with ball. Neither reluctant master nor Mason gains any satisfaction from the game, since one immediately quits and the other is wondering why no one will throw the ball for him.

Keep in mind that I am not the master here. The master is my wife, who has vainly attempted for many years to get Mason to play a real game of fetch. On occasion, he may go after the ball and even bring it part way back, but never has he actually chased the ball, caught it, and then obediently returned and dropped it at her feet. He's still learning.

At our house, we like to play card games. Solitaire, Peanuts, and Texas Hold 'em are among our favorites. We usually play on the living room floor, which of course brings us to dog-level and gets Mason all excited. The moment he hears the slapping of cards he comes running.

As the game begins, he runs to find his favorite chew toy, which as of this writing is a ring painted to look like a doughnut from Dunkin Donuts. He brings the doughnut to whoever is closest, which of course is always me, and drops it with that expectant look on his face. I whip the toy across the room, appearing as if I'm playing his game but actually doing it only to get him away from me. Of course, unlike playing outdoors with the tennis ball, Mason faithfully brings the doughnut right back and drops it in my lap. He knows that I don't care about playing fetch when I'm playing cards, so he plays the game correctly, just to be contrary.

No card game is complete without someone coming to the door. When the doorbell rings, the doughnut gets dropped, and Mason runs full tilt through the card game, leaving cards strewn everywhere in his wake. Doorbell plus cards is never a good combination.

Like any dog, Mason has an innate killer instinct that emerges from time to time. A dog walking on the other side of the street prompts Mason to pump up his chest, prance around, and snarl. But if the dog so much as looks at Mason, our little pugilist cowers and backs off. Another example of this killer instinct is when he finds a dead bird. Up until the moment he realizes it's dead, he tries to beat the bird into submission.

But the family favorite of all of Mason's antics is when he spots a squirrel. We have several ground-level windows, so he has a commanding view of the deck, yard, and surrounding area. We also have several towering oak trees in our yard, which means there are always squirrels running about.

Mason hates squirrels. Nothing will get him barking, growling, and in a tizzy as much as seeing a squirrel. While it isn't possible for any dog, let alone Mason, to catch a squirrel, he keeps trying. For eight years now he's been chasing squirrels with a continued intensity that makes it clear that he actually thinks he'll catch one. The dog has the speed of Underdog when he spots a squirrel, at least until he reaches the sliding glass door. Most of the time he stops when he gets there, prancing in place until someone opens it. He has been known, however, to run top speed into the door, effectively ending the chase before it's begun and giving him a good reason to lie down for the rest of the day.

If he does make it outside, he runs in place trying to get

traction on the plastic deck surface, looking for all the world like Fred Flintstone struggling to get the car moving. By the time Mason does get forward momentum, the squirrel is three houses down. But he never seems disappointed at not getting the squirrel. In fact, he seems quite pleased that he chased the menacing creature away, returning with tail wagging as if he's done us all a favor. Just once, I would like to see the squirrel come back wagging its tail, with Mason running away.

For entertainment, we'll quietly open the door when we see a squirrel that Mason hasn't yet noticed. Then, picking him up so as not to let him see the prey, we fling him out the door toward the squirrel, yelling, "Go get 'em, Mason!" To which the dog responds hitting the ground at a full run before seeing where the squirrel actually is.

The squirrels have gotten to know Mason, not as a threat but as an annoyance that disturbs their quiet existence. (The squirrels and I are much alike in that regard.) When Mason is circling the yard for an appropriate place to pee, you often hear a squirrel overhead, chattering away at him, clearly peeved at his presence.

NEAR DEATH EXPERIENCE

The summer after we nearly lost Mason to the waves of Lake Michigan, there came another brush with death for the dog. This time, it was not due to Mason's stupidity or his natural tendency toward the dramatic but was rather due to natural causes. It was in the middle of winter, and Mason began to get very lethargic. He's not an overly energetic dog in the first place, but he was noticeably slowing down; it was clear that something was wrong. He started eating less, and when he did eat, he would often throw most of it up. He lost three pounds in short order, which may not seem like much except that he started out at twelve pounds. There was also a noticeable increase in peeing around the house, *if that could be possible*. There was one upside to his distress; his decrease in food intake led to a corresponding decrease in his pooping around the house. However, he was definitely sick, and even I didn't like to see the poor dog suffer.

Cindy called the vet, and he suggested a prescription to help Mason digest his food better. Just the idea of a dog prescription made me laugh, and I knew that we were about to embark on one of those dog medical missions I vowed I'd never pursue. It occurred to me that a prescription intended to help break down the food for a dog with a natural tendency to puke and poop around the house didn't seem like a good idea. It seemed to me that we were trading one bad proposition for one that was worse, and neither outcome was pleasant for me. Still, a healthy dog with issues that have become predicable and accepted outweighed a sick dog who would become a money pit that puked and peed without warning. We gave Mason the prescription in the hopes of bringing the dog back to health.

After a couple of weeks, there was no improvement, and another call to the vet made it unavoidable that we would have to bring him in and have his blood drawn for lab work. There was a problem in drawing blood, however, because blood draw and lab work were going to cost $180—considerably above the $125 spending limit that had been set years ago. Only weeks earlier, I had my annual physical and the lab work for me was $160, which, to say the least, seems a bit strange. (I wish someone could explain to me why lab-work, checkups and dental cleanings on twelve-pound dogs cost more than they do for two hundred pound people.) Rather than make an issue out of it, I have resigned myself to this injustice, yet another in a string of inequities between dogs and people.

When told of the budgetary dilemma, the gracious vet said we could bring Mason in for a general go-over and perhaps that would reveal something. The cost of the go-over was $55, well within the dog medical budget, so we—I should say Cindy—brought Mason to the vet on her way to work. Since she had to work that day and I was at home, she informed me that I would have to pick up Mason when the vet was finished with him. She knew this was like asking me to clean toilets, so to soften the chore, Cindy offered to pay the $55 from her slush fund, which made the task more palatable for me. There was also an automatic assumption, at least on my part, that there would be an additional quid pro quo payment in my not too distant future.

Putting Mason in a car is an unpleasant and outright dangerous thing. In addition to his whining and jumping over every square inch of the car, you have to constantly watch that he won't relieve himself in his excitement. In the past, I have tried to shove him onto the floor, which solves both the jumping around and excrement problem, but holding him there can be distracting. The last thing I want is to die in a car accident with Mason because of his antics. The thought of the obituary makes me cringe: "Man Who Really Hated His Dog Dies Trying to Save Dog's Life Returning from Vet." The ultimate irony for me would be to have been known as the guy who died trying to save the very dog that everyone knew he had hoped would die.

The vet called late in the day and said Mason was ready to be picked up. Conversations with the vet are never short affairs, and I think that is because they are trained to go overboard on the emotional aspects of treating people's pets. One of the things people working in veterinary offices are taught is to talk about the pet as though it were a person. They discuss the problem, but in a very caring and overly emotional way as if to say they are aware of the emotional trauma the pet owner is going through. They always refer to the pet in the first person, trying to say the dog's name as often as possible, alternating between talking to you and the dog. "Mason has a sore tummy that is making little Mason hurt very much; don't you, Mason? Mason is so sweet, but we don't like it when little Mason doesn't feel well; do we, Mason? These pills should help little Mason feel better soon, and, Mason, you need to take these like a good puppy; okay, Mason?" The whole conversation is enough to make me puke on spot. The veterinarian apparently had no idea that I was the last person in the world who wanted to talk emotionally about their dog, but then I think that I am the exception to the rule. Most dog owners love that sort of attention and take comfort in having a vet that cares enough to talk directly to the animal. I didn't have the heart to interject and say that I really couldn't care less, so I listened to the diagnosis as patiently as I could.

I went to pick up Mason, and they greeted me like a rock star when I walked into the office. I will say this about veterinary clinics, animal shelters, and grooming centers; you are treated like royalty because you are considered to be in the fraternity of dog lovers. Again, I didn't have the heart to share my views on dogs; besides, some of these people are so over the top that I would fear for my life if I uttered any sort of derogatory comment against my dog. I paid the bill and then watched as they affectionately paraded Mason out to who they assumed was the happy owner. One of the things I really hate about the dog-loving world is how they refer to dog owners as either mommy or daddy. "Mason, here is your daddy to pick you up," they say in a syrupy voice. They never said that when we took our kids in for checkups when they were young (yet another example of the dog and people worlds being totally out of sync in the dog-lovers mind).

I was told in minute detail every aspect of Mason's illness, and it wasn't pretty. Mason had a bladder infection caused by a ph imbalance in his urine. Said infection was induced by an obstruction in the urinary tract caused by matted hair lodged in the urethra. Furthermore, "the penis shaft was bent over at a ninety-degree angle making urination difficult and uncomfortable." They removed the obstructions, trimmed away hair from the affected area and ostensibly straightened out the penis, although I don't understand how they do that any more than I understand how the thing got bent in the first place. All of this for $55, which, I have to say, sounds like a deal to me, especially considering the conditions under which the doctor had to work.

I patiently listed to another summation of Mason's illness while feigning interest and then got out of there. Besides, I was a little disgruntled because they hadn't said that the best thing to do was to put him down. One additional piece of information was given; Mason seemed to act strangely with his food while at the vet. He would look at his food and try to tip it out of the dog dish. He then tried to cover it with the dog dish while not eating any of it. This really baffled the vet, who referred to the behavior as obsessive and compulsive. I, of course, had seen it all before and was not the least bit surprised by Mason's eccentric behavior.

The ride home was more humorous than it was annoying. Mason tried to jump around but was still under the influence of the anesthesia they used when straightening out his penis. He couldn't walk straight enough to get to my side of the car, and in fact, fell off the seat and didn't have the coordination to get back up again. I left him on the floor where he couldn't bother me. The effect of anesthesia on a dog is a funny thing and much different than the effect on people. Since people talk, they tend to slur words, say stupid things and curse a bit more freely than usual. Dogs can't talk, but they compensate in their locomotion skills. When Mason got home he began wandering aimlessly around the house, bumping into walls, furniture, and people. He'd bump into something and simply move on, acting as if the bump pointed him in a new direction. He reminded me of one of those robotic vacuum cleaners that changes direction by bumping into something. He would also yip in an uncontrolled but weak manner. It seemed to be almost unintentional as he would stop wandering, stand in the middle of the kitchen, and just let out a yip every twenty seconds or so. He would do that for five minutes and then stop as suddenly as he started.

When Cindy arrived home from work, I had to fill her in on all that had transpired that afternoon. Unlike me, she genuinely cared for the dog's wellbeing and was very concerned about what the doctor had to say. I explained everything that the vet had told me, but when I got to the part about the bent penis, Cindy started to cry. She was all concerned that the stopped-up plumbing was partially her fault and that she should have noticed something like that. She felt that in the course of tummy rubs she had full view of everything Mason, so in her mind that would have been noticeable. Of course, a penis the size of a broken toothpick isn't that noticeable, especially when covered by so much dog hair, but she had it in her head that she should have noticed the problem.

The vet had given us another prescription, this one an appetite stimulant that would hopefully cause him to eat more and put on some weight. I was getting the feeling that this was a trial and error approach to medicine, but after my history with Mason, nothing surprised me anymore. After a couple of days, Mason began behaving more strangely than usual. He was still wandering around the house aimlessly, but now he would stop in front of a wall and just stare at it. He would stand there for minutes, blankly staring at the wall. He would then move on and try to jump on the couch, which couldn't happen because he wasn't able to align himself perpendicular with the couch. This was strange behavior, even for Mason, and Cindy again called the vet thinking that maybe the anesthesia was still having an effect four days later. Mason, on the other hand, was genuinely entertaining me, for the first time since the calendar came out.

The vet said that no, the anesthesia could not still be affecting Mason four days later. Instead, likely the antidepressants, which were part of the appetite stimulant pills, were the culprit. I would really like to know what compelled someone to develop an antidepressant for a dog, and I would also like to know how one tells that a dog is depressed. Frankly, I don't know how on earth a dog could be depressed, they don't do anything except eat, play and sleep. Again, I kept my views to myself. They advised us to take him off those pills and again bring him in, this time for a more in-depth evaluation. Of course, this would mean that we were going to be over the budget, but Cindy said that she would pick up the tab with her money. I suspect she was still feeling guilty about the bent penis and an in-depth evaluation by the vet would assuage her guilt somewhat.

We went through the routine again, Cindy bringing him to the vet and me picking him up. This time they gave Mason an extensive evaluation, including blood work and an X-ray of his innards. I again received the call that Mason was ready to be picked up so I went in, paid the $200 bill with Cindy's money, and listened to the "Mason, here is your daddy" routine prior to getting down to hearing the diagnosis. I was told that Mason's was a unique case. They performed all of the necessary tests only to discover that they had no idea what was wrong with Mason. I was sure glad that Cindy was paying for this. While they were unable to determine why he wasn't eating, they did discover that Mason had an exceptionally enlarged heart, no doubt because of the intense love the dog felt for me. Of course, I left the veterinary clinic with some pills to deal with the enlarged heart, which had absolutely nothing to do with what was wrong with him. The doctor said that the next step, should we want to proceed, would be to take him to Grand Rapids and have a more extensive MRI done on the dog. This was too much for even Cindy's budget, and the $255 she had already spent helped her sleep well knowing that she had done nearly all she could do to help the poor dog. Mason gradually improved, and while we don't know what he had or how he got better, we ended up right back where we started; a predictable routine of the three P's and a mutual understanding between Mason and me that we would grudgingly tolerate each other.

RECONCILIATION

Mason bugs me in many ways, but I think the thing that bothers me the most is why he likes me so much. The entire family would agree that Mason likes me the best. My older son refers to it as the "alpha male" syndrome. My wife thinks he is trying to win my approval. My daughter thinks he's scared of me and is being submissive, and my younger son thinks I am imagining the whole thing.

Whatever the reasons, it is quite clear to most that the dog likes me better than anyone else, and it doesn't make any sense. When I sit on the couch, he sits by my feet on the footstool. If I lie outside in the lounge chair, Mason lies underneath. When I come home from travel, he's there to greet me as if he couldn't wait for me to get home. When we play cards on the floor, he brings the chew toy to me first.

Some will say, "Oh, isn't that sweet," or tell me that I should appreciate such love. But I do not nor will I ever appreciate his affections. In the first place, he is always kissing up to me because of something he did to upset me. Whether he did a Three P or in some other way inconvenienced my life, he's trying to make amends. If I accept his affection, he'll all the more quickly do something to displease me again. It's his strategy to keep the family loving him and thereby reap the benefits of health and home from me. He has me right where he wants me, and he knows it.

True Mason-lovers

It has now been eight long years through which I've had to endure this dog. Despite the friction, anger, and disdain, Mason and I have developed a mutual tolerance of each other. He feigns that he likes me, and I readily admit that I don't like him. If I give him his space, however, he appears to respond by behaving a little better. In turn, if he withholds bodily fluids and noisy tirades, I do my best not to entirely disregard his presence. As long as we stay within the boundaries of mutual tolerance and as long as my wife doesn't go away overnight, we're able to muddle through.

One thing I will not deny is that pets—and dogs in particular—become part of the family, for better or for worse. To the beyond reason dog lover, they are one of the children, and they receive equal rights. To me, the dog is like grease on the garage floor: not something you want but not entirely objectionable either. It is just a garage, after all.

When I am alone on the deck having my evening cigar, Mason will come up to me, reach his front paws to my knees and stretch. It is a small and insignificant gesture that I entirely ignore but completely understand. After all these years, Mason and I have developed an understanding that is beyond words and affection. It's his way of thanking me for allowing him to live at our house, and by not pushing him away, I am showing acceptance of his thanks.

Contrary to what some people might think, I'm not entirely heartless. No one else witnesses that pat on the head he receives in the morning on my way to work, or the times I let him out when no one knows. I've even been known to throw him a scrap of food when no one is looking. It doesn't hurt my pride or image to rub his ears before I go to bed, as long as nobody else sees it. It is part of the evolved reality, and what is necessary to keep the peace between us.

I don't receive a tale wag, lick, or other canine affection for my actions, and that's the way I want it. And in turn, I don't acknowledge him when he lies at my feet or nuzzles my hand. He wouldn't dare try to sit on my lap, but he does get close enough to touch my leg. Our mutual relationship of tolerance won't allow certain boundaries to be crossed, and the fact that we both understand it is the basis for our mutual respect.

Dogs live well beyond eight years, and Murphy's Law dictates that Mason will live until he's fifteen; you can count on it. Knowing this, we will continue our existence of accommodation until the end. I have just now patted him on the head "good night," and with that, I am finished with my diatribe. If Mason were to die tonight, I would feel no loss, and I have no doubt the feeling is mutual. Odds are that he will go first, though, and when he does, we most definitely will *not* be getting another dog.

Once we're both gone, I suspect that after I answer to God for my treatment of Mason, the dog will wander up and greet me as a long lost friend. Since all things are perfect in heaven, and since we are told that the lion will lie down with the lamb, I won't speculate on what my relationship with Mason will be at that time. It's safe to say, however, that he'll be the perfect dog, and therefore will be far more tolerable.

Until then, Mason and I take one day at a time as we share this home together. There will continue to be issues between us; I have no doubt about that. Just today, there was another incident of one of the Three Ps, and as usual I pointed it out and my wife cleaned it up. I glared at Mason and he cowered, but there was no yelling or discipline involved as in the past. At this point it wouldn't serve any purpose. Two of the three kids are off to college, so I don't have as much pressure to love the dog, which makes it easier to simply ignore him.

Initially, the notion of Mason or Me was an ultimatum, a choice between who stayed and who left. I learned long ago, however, that that interpretation would not work in my favor. Mason or Me has now come to mean who is ultimately in charge of the Mouw household. The true answer is nebulous, based upon who is being asked, but if you were to ask me, Mason is the ultimate winner in this conflict. Every time he looks at me with that blinkless stare, there is a gleam in his eyes that tells me that he knows it too.

AFTERWORD

The problems Mason was experiencing due to his enlarged heart became worse in the months leading up to publication of this book. The vet indicated that there was little that could be done, and things would have to run their course. We were assured that he was not in pain, so we enjoyed Mason as long as we could. We had hoped that he would live long enough for our two oldest children to say goodbye when they were home from college for spring break, but he did not last that long.

One evening in early spring, Mason and I were home alone together. He was moving very slowly, and his breathing was becoming labored. The family knew it was getting near the end, and we planned to take him in the next morning to have the vet put him down. Knowing this was our last night together, I thought it only fitting that I do some bonding with Mason, especially since it was just he and I alone. At his stage, I knew no one would fault me for loving on the dog, but it was certainly more comfortable for me doing so with no one else around.

I reclined on the floor and called Mason. He slowly walked over and stood the customary distance away from me. I reached over and started rubbing his neck, slowly nudging him closer to me. Soon he was leaning up against me, visibly surprised at the attention he was getting from me yet clearly enjoying it. I gently forced him into a lying position and whispered the once unthinkable, "Mason want a tummy rub?" He slowly rolled over, and I gave him the long, gentle tummy rub he had previously been denied.

As I rubbed his tummy, he looked straight at me and began licking my arm. We lay together a while before he needed to get up, but in that brief encounter, we both knew we had said our good-byes.

Mason died later that night, and some may think it ironic that he and I were the ones to have the most affectionate farewell, but it didn't seem at all surprising to Mason or me. Good-bye, my nemesis and friend, I will miss you.